singing for mrs. pettigrew

singing for mrs. pettigrew

stories and essays from a writing life

michael morpurgo

illustrated by peter bailey

CANDLEWICK PRESS

Text copyright © 2006 by Michael Morpurgo
Illustrations copyright © 2006 by Peter Bailey

Meeting Cézanne was first broadcast May 2004 on BBC Radio 4; first published in 2005
by Hay Festival Press. "The Giant's Necklace" is taken from *The White Horse of Zennor
and Other Stories*, first published in 1982 by Egmont Books. *I Believe in Unicorns* was first
published in 2004 as a short story in *The Times* (London); a longer version was published
in 2005 by Walker Books Ltd. "My One and Only Great Escape" is taken from *Ten of
the Best School Stories with a Difference!*, first published in 2002 by HarperCollins
Publishers. "My Father Is a Polar Bear" is taken from *From Hereabout Hill*, first published
in 2000 by Egmont Books. *The Silver Swan* was first published in 2000 by Doubleday.
"What Does It Feel Like?" is taken from *From Hereabout Hill*, first published in 2000 by
Egmont Books. "Half a Man" is taken from *War*, first published in 2005 by Pan
Macmillan. "For Carlos, A Letter from Your Father" is taken from *Lines in the Sand*, first
published in 2003 by Frances Lincoln Limited.

"Last Load" from *Collected Poems* by Ted Hughes. Copyright © 2003 by the Estate of
Ted Hughes. Reprinted by permission of Farrar, Straus and Giroux, LLC.

"I Speak of a Valley" from *Poems* by Sean Rafferty, published by etruscan books and
used by permission of Christian Coupe.

First U.S. edition 2009

Library of Congress Cataloging-in-Publication Data is available.

Library of Congress Catalog Card Number 2008938403

ISBN 978-0-7636-3624-1

2 4 6 8 10 9 7 5 3 1

Printed in the United States of America

This book has been typeset in Poliphilus and Blado.

Candlewick Press
99 Dover Street
Somerville, Massachusetts 02144

visit us at www.candlewick.com

contents

explain yourself: an introduction

"Explain yourself, Morpurgo." I was asked to do this quite often when I was at school. The trick, of course, was to come up with an excuse that would get me out of trouble. I became rather good at this, I think, probably because I had to be. It was a question of survival, a very necessary technique that most of us have had to master in our time.

In this book I am not excusing myself, but I am trying to explain myself, to understand why and how I write what I do. I shall try to explain myself to myself and in so doing will, I hope, explain myself to you.

Why trouble? Why should a writer seek to explain his craft to his readers? What's the point? Surely the stories them-selves are all you need? Surely it's through reading these that we can come to an understanding of a writer's mind and methodology? That would seem to be true. It should be sufficient. This is why you will find in this book more stories than anything else. However, there are those who would like to probe a little deeper, who are not happy simply to gaze at the field of ripe wheat dancing in the breeze and wonder. They want to understand how a single grain of wheat grows, from where the seed comes, how it is planted and fertilized, how the earth cradles it, how the sun and rain sustain it. Perhaps this insight can lead to a more profound appreciation of the stories themselves, but more importantly it may give the reader the idea that this process of story/making and story/telling is for everyone, that we all of us have the seeds of stories inside us, that it is simply a question of planting it and encouraging it to grow.

I am a grower of stories. I farm them as surely as a farmer does his wheat. I am a weaver of dreams, a teller of tales. I have, through my mother reading to me; through my own reading; through inspired teachers; through my great mentors Robert Louis Stevenson, Ted Hughes, and Sean Rafferty; through years of practice, discovered my way of doing it. Every writer's way is unique, I am sure, though perhaps we all have much more in common than we believe. My way will not be the only way, but it is my way, and I hope it might be interesting and maybe even useful and encouraging to tell the story of how I became the writer I am.

That is what I have tried to do in this book. I have woven some of my stories and essays — many of them written during my years as Britain's Children's Laureate, from 2003 to 2005 — in such a way that the one enlightens the other, informs the other, complements the other. It is not the story of my life — that is for another time maybe — but it is the story of this writer's story/making journey. ➤

meeting cézanne

I don't remember why my mother had to go into the hospital. I'm not sure she ever told me. She did explain that after the operation she would need a month of complete rest. This was why she had to arrange for me to go and stay with Aunt Mathilde, my mother's older sister, in her house down in the south, in Provence.

I'd never been to Provence, but I had met my aunt Mathilde a few times when she'd come to see us in our little apartment in Paris. I remembered her being big and bustling, filling the place with her bulk and forever hugging and kissing me, which I never much cared for. She'd pinch my cheek and tell me I was a "beau-tiful little man." But she'd always bring us lots of crystallized fruits, so I could forgive her everything else.

I was ten years old and had never been parted from my mother. I'd only been out of Paris once for a vacation by the sea in

Brittany. I told her I didn't want to be sent away. I told her time and again, but it was no use.

"You'll be fine, Yannick," she insisted. "You like Aunt Mathilde, don't you? And Uncle Bruno is very funny. He has a mustache that prickles like a hedgehog. And you've never even met your cousin Amandine. You'll have a lovely time. Spring in Provence. It'll be a paradise for you, I promise. Crystallized fruit every day!"

She did all she could to convince me. More than once she read me Jean Giono's story "The Man Who Planted Trees," the story of an old shepherd, set in the high hills of Provence. She showed me a book of paintings by Paul Cézanne—paintings, she told me, of the countryside outside Aix-en-Provence, very close to Aunt Mathilde's home. "Isn't it beautiful, Yannick?" she breathed as she turned the pages. "Cézanne loved it there, and he's the great-est painter in the world. Remember that."

A city boy all my life, the paintings really did look like the paradise my mother had promised me. So by the time she put me on the train at the Gare de Lyon, I was really looking forward to it. Blowing kisses to her for the last time out the train window, I think the only reason I didn't cry was because I was quite sure by now that I was indeed going to the most wonderful place in the world—the place where Cézanne, the greatest painter in the world, painted his pictures, where Jean Giono's old shepherd walked the high wild hills planting his acorns to make a forest. Aunt Mathilde met me at the train and enveloped me in a great bear hug and pinched my cheek. It wasn't a good start. She introduced me to my cousin Amandine, who barely acknowledged my existence, but who was very beautiful. On the way to the car, following behind Aunt Mathilde, Amandine told me at once that she was fourteen and much older than I was and that I had to do what she said. I loved her at once. She wore a blue-and-white gingham dress, and she had a ponytail of chestnut hair that shone in the sunshine. She had the greenest eyes I'd ever seen. She didn't smile at me, though. I hoped that one day she would.

We drove out of town to Vauvenargues, Aunt Mathilde talking all the way. I was in the backseat of the Deux Chevaux and couldn't hear everything, but I did pick up enough to understand that Uncle Bruno ran the village inn. He did the cooking and everyone helped. "And you'll have to help, too," Amandine added without even turning to look at me. Everywhere about me were the gentle hills and folding valleys, the little houses and dark, pointing trees I'd seen in Cézanne's paintings. Uncle

Bruno greeted me, wrapped in his white apron. Mother was right. He did have a huge hedgehog of a mustache that prickled when he kissed me. I liked him at once.

I had my own little room above the restaurant, looking out over a small back garden. An almond tree grew there, the pink blossoms brushing against my windowpane. Beyond the tree were the hills, Cézanne's hills. And after supper they gave me a crystallized fruit: apricot, my favorite. All that and Amandine, too. I could not have been happier.

It became clear to me very quickly that while I was made to feel very welcome and part of the family—Aunt Mathilde was always showing me off proudly to her customers as her nephew, "her beautiful little man from Paris"—I was indeed expected to do what everyone else did, to do my share of the work in the inn. Uncle Bruno was almost always busy in his kitchen. He clanked his pots and sang his songs, and would waggle his mustache at me whenever I went in, which always made me giggle. He was happiest in his kitchen; I could tell that. Aunt Mathilde bustled and hustled; she liked things to be just so. She greeted every customer like a long-lost friend. She was the heart and soul of the place. As for Amandine, she took me in hand at once and explained that I'd be working with her, that she'd been asked to look after me. She did not mince her words. I could not expect to spend my summer with them, she said, and not earn my keep.

She put me to work at once in the restaurant: setting tables, clearing tables, cutting bread, filling up breadbaskets, filling carafes of water, making sure there was enough wood on the fire in the evenings, and washing up, of course. After just one day I was exhausted. Amandine told me I had to learn to work harder and faster, but she did kiss me good night before I went upstairs, which was why I did not wash my face for days afterward.

At least I had the mornings to myself. I made the best of the time I had, exploring the hills, stomping through the woods, climb-ing trees. Amandine never came with me. She had lots of friends in the village, bigger boys who stood about with their thumbs hooked into the pockets of their blue jeans and roared around on motor scooters with Amandine clinging on behind, her hair flying. These were the boys she smiled at, the boys she laughed with. I was more sad than jealous, I think; I simply loved her more than ever.

There was a routine to the restaurant work. As soon as the cus-tomers had left, Amandine would take away the wineglasses and the bottles and the carafes. The coffee cups and the cutlery were my job. She would deal with the ashtrays, while I scrunched up the paper tablecloths and threw them on the fire. Then we'd set the table again as quickly as possible for the next guests. I worked hard because I wanted to please Amandine and make her smile at me. She never did.

She laughed at me, though. She was in the village street one morning, her motor-scooter friends gathered adoringly all around her, when she turned and saw me. They all did. Then she was laughing, and they were, too. I walked away knowing I should be hating her, but I couldn't. I longed all the more for her smile. I longed for her just to notice me. With every day she didn't, I became more and more miserable, sometimes so wretched I would cry myself to sleep at nights. I lived for my mother's letters and for my morning walks in the hills that Cézanne had painted, gathering acorns from the trees Jean Giono's old shepherd had planted. There, away from Amandine's indifference, I could be happy for a while and dream my dreams. I thought that one day I might like to live in these hills myself and be a painter like Cézanne, the greatest painter in the world, or maybe a wonderful writer like Jean Giono.

I think Uncle Bruno sensed my unhappiness because he began to take me more and more under his wing. He'd often invite me into his kitchen and let me help him cook his *soupe au pistou* or his *poulet romarin* with *pommes dauphinoises* and wild leeks.

He taught me to make chocolate mousse and *crème brûlée*, and before I left he'd always waggle his mustache for me and give me a crystallized apricot. But I dreaded the restaurant now, dreaded having to face Amandine again and endure the silence between us. I dreaded it, but would not have missed it for the world. I loved her that much.

Then one day a few weeks later I got a letter from my mother saying she was much better now, that Aunt Mathilde would put me on the train home in a few days' time. I was torn. Of course I yearned to be home again, to see my mother, but at the same time I did not want to leave Amandine.

That evening Amandine told me I had to do everything just right because their best customer was coming to dine with some friends. He lived in the château in the village, she said, and was very famous, but when I asked what he was famous for, she didn't seem interested in telling me.

"Questions, always questions." She tutted. "Go and fetch the logs."

Whoever he was, he looked ordinary enough to me, just an old man with not much hair. But he ate one of the *crème brûlées* I'd made, and I felt very pleased a famous man had eaten one of my *crème brûlées*. As soon as he and his friends had gone, we began to clear the table. I pulled the paper tablecloth off as usual, and as usual scrunched it up and threw it on the fire. Suddenly Amandine was rushing past me. For some reason I could not understand at all, she grabbed the tongs and tried to pull the remnants of the burning paper tablecloth out of the flames, but it was already too late. Then she turned on me.

"You fool!" she shouted. "You little fool."

"What?" I said.

"That man who just left. If he likes his meal he does a drawing on the tablecloth for Papa as a tip, and you've gone and thrown it on the fire. He's only the most famous painter in the world. Idiot! Imbecile!" She was in tears now. Everyone in the restaurant had stopped eating and gone quite silent.

Then Uncle Bruno was striding toward us, not his jolly self at all. "What is it?" he asked Amandine. "What's the matter?"

"It was Yannick, Papa," she cried. "He threw it on the fire — the tablecloth, the drawing."

"Had you told him about it, Amandine?" Uncle Bruno asked. "Did Yannick know about how sometimes he sketches something on the tablecloth, and how he leaves it behind for us?"

Amandine looked at me, her cheeks wet with tears. I thought she was going to lie. But she didn't.

"No, Papa," she said, lowering her head.

"Then you shouldn't be blaming him, should you, for something that was your fault. Say sorry to Yannick now." She mumbled it but she never raised her eyes. Uncle Bruno put his arm around me and walked me away. "Never mind, Yannick," he said. "He said he particularly liked his *crème brûlée*. That's probably why he left the drawing. You made the *crème brûlée*, didn't you? So it was for you, really, he did it. Always look on the bright side. For a moment you had in your hands a drawing done for you and your *crème brûlée* by the greatest painter in the world. That's something you'll never forget."

Later on as I came out of the bathroom, I heard Amandine crying in her room. I hated to hear her crying, so I knocked on the door and went in. She was lying curled up on her bed, hugging her pillow.

"I'm sorry," I said. "I didn't mean to upset you." She had stopped crying by now.

"It wasn't your fault, Yannick," she said, still sniffling a bit. "It's just that I hate it when Papa's cross with me. He hardly ever is, only when I've done something really bad. I shouldn't have blamed you. I'm sorry."

And then she smiled at me. Amandine smiled at me!

I lay awake all that night, my mind racing. Somehow I was going to put it all right again. I was going to make Amandine happy. By morning I had worked out exactly what I had to do and how to do it, even what I was going to say when the time came.

That morning, I didn't go for my walk in the hills. Instead I made my way down through the village toward the château. I'd often wondered what it was like behind those closed gates. Now I was going to find out. I waited till there was no one about, no cars coming. I climbed the gates easily enough, then ran down through the trees. And there it was, immense and forbidding, surrounded by forest on all sides. And there he was, the old man with very little hair whom I had seen the night before. He was sitting alone in the sunshine at the foot of the steps in front of the château, and he was sketching. I approached as silently as I could across the grass, but somehow I must have disturbed him. He looked up, shading his eyes against the sun. "Hello, young man," he said. Now that I was this close to him, I could see he was indeed old, very old, but his eyes were young and bright and searching.

"Are you Monsieur Cézanne?" I asked him. "Are you the famous painter?" He seemed a little puzzled at this, so I went on. "My mother says you are the greatest painter in the world."

He was smiling now, then laughing. "I think your mother's

He was sitting alone in the sunshine in front of the château, and he was sketching.

probably right," he said. "You clearly have a wise mother, but what I'd like to know is why she let a young lad like you come wandering here on his own."

As I explained everything and told him why I'd come and what I wanted, he looked at me very intently, his brow furrowing. "I remember you now, from last night," he said when I'd finished. "Of course I'll draw another picture for Bruno. What would he like? No. Better still, what would you like?"

"I like sailing boats," I told him. "Can you do boats?"

"I'll try," he replied with a smile.

It didn't take him long. He drew fast, never once looking up. But he did ask me questions as he worked, about where I'd seen sailing boats, about where I lived in Paris. He loved Paris, he said, and he loved sailing boats, too.

"There," he said, tearing the sheet from his sketchbook and showing me. "What do you think?" Four sailing boats were racing over the sea out beyond a lighthouse, just as I'd seen them in Brittany. But I saw he'd signed it *Picasso*.

"I thought your name was Cézanne," I said.

He smiled up at me. "How I wish it were," he said sadly. "How I wish it were. Off you go now."

I ran all the way back to the village, wishing all the time that

I'd told him that I was the one who had made the *crème brûlée* he'd liked so much. I found Amandine by the clothesline, a clothes-pin in her mouth. "I did it!" I cried breathlessly, waving the drawing at her. "I did it! To make up for the one I burned."

Amandine took the pin out of her mouth and looked down at the drawing.

"That's really sweet of you to try, Yannick," she said. "But the thing is, it's got to be done by him, by Picasso himself. It's no good you drawing a picture and then just signing his name. It's got to be by him or it's not worth any money."

I was speechless. Then as she turned away to hang up one of Uncle Bruno's aprons, Aunt Mathilde came out into the garden with a basket of washing under her arm.

"Yannick's been very kind, Maman," Amandine said. "He's made me a drawing. After what happened last night. It's really good, too."

Aunt Mathilde had put down her washing and was looking at the drawing. "Bruno!" she called. "Bruno, come out here!" And Uncle Bruno appeared, his hands white with flour. "Look at this," said Aunt Mathilde. "Look what Yannick did, and all by himself, too."

Bruno peered at it closely for a moment, then started to roar with laughter. "I don't think so," he said. "Yannick may be a genius with *crème brûlée,* but this is by Picasso, the great man himself. I promise you. Isn't it, Yannick?"

So I told them the whole story. When I'd finished, Amandine came over and hugged me. She had tears in her eyes. I was in seventh heaven, and Uncle Bruno waggled his mustache and gave me six crystallized apricots. Unfortunately Aunt Mathilde hugged me, too, and pinched my cheek especially hard. I was the talk of the inn that night and felt very proud of myself. But best of all, Amandine came with me on my walk in the hills the next day and climbed trees with me and collected acorns, and held my hand all the way back down the village street, where everyone could see us, even the motor-scooter boys in their blue jeans.

They still have the boat drawing by Picasso hanging in the inn. Amandine runs the place now. It's as good as ever. She married someone else, as cousins usually do. So did I. I'm a writer, still trying to follow in Jean Giono's footsteps. As for Cézanne, was my mother right? Is he the greatest painter in the world? Or is it Picasso? Who knows? Who cares? They're both wonderful, and I've met both of them—if you see what I'm saying. ✢

an art and a craft and a marvelous magic

A certain fear of the empty page has stayed with me since my school days. For me it still seems to perfectly mirror an empty mind bereft of ideas. It saps my confidence and my will and any hope I might be harboring that I can cover the page with words at all, let alone with a coherent story. Yet almost every day of my life I choose to face down that fear. It is not because I am brave. Rather, I am like a sailor who knows the terror of the sea and has discovered over the years and after countless voyages and adventures that the only way to banish this terror is by knowing and understanding the sea in all its moods so well that he is no longer frustrated when becalmed, nor terrified for his life in the midst of the storm. And just as a sailor goes out once again to face the perils of the open sea, so I go to my bed each day, pile up my pillows behind me, settle back, pick up a pen, draw up my knees, open the exercise book, and confront once more the open sea of the empty page. The mariner sails the sea because he longs to, because it is a challenge he needs, because each time he is testing himself, exploring, discovering. I write for the same reason.

But my need to write has another motivation too, one I share in part at least with sailors, I think. I like to feel connected—to myself, to my memory, to the world about me, to my readers. It is, I suppose, my way of feeling most intensely that I belong.

I have often wondered in four decades of writing how it is that time and again my stories seem to gather themselves, write themselves almost (the best ones really seem to), cover the empty pages almost effortlessly—once I get going, that is. Each one is, I believe, the result of forces of a creative fusion, a fusion that simply can't happen unless certain elements are in place, a fusion I don't properly understand, but can only guess at. But it is an informed guess.

At the core of it, without which there would simply never have been any fusion at all, is the life I have lived: as a child in London; as a son and a brother on the Essex coast; away at boarding school; then as a soldier; a student; a husband; a father; a teacher; farmer; traveler; lecturer; storyteller; grandfather. I didn't live this life in order to write stories, of course—for at least half my life I had no idea I even wanted to write—but without its joys and its pain, its highs and its lows, I would have precious little to write about and probably no desire to write anyway.

For me, memory is the source material that is needed for this fusion—the memory of falling off a bike into a ditch ("Singing for Mrs. Pettigrew"); of being cast away on an island in Scilly (*Why the Whales Came, Kensuke's Kingdom*); of collecting cowrie shells on a beach near Zennor ("The Giant's Necklace"); of running away from boarding school (*The Butterfly Lion*, "My One and Only Great Escape"); of a family friend terribly scarred when he was shot down in the RAF in the war ("Half a Man"); of seeing my father for the first time in my life ("My Father Is a Polar Bear"); of loving

the paintings of Cézanne (*Meeting Cézanne*) and the music of
Mozart, the poetry of Ted Hughes (*The Silver Swan*) and the
stories of Robert Louis Stevenson (*I Believe in Unicorns*); of a
small boy sitting entranced on his tricycle in a square in
Venice at ten o'clock at night, watching a violinist play in the
street (*The Mozart Question*); of a village divided over the con-
struction of an atomic power station; of a lady who lived in a
railway car near the sea and gave me a glass of milk and a jam
sandwich when I was little; and of a single lark rising into the
blue ("Singing for Mrs. Pettigrew"). So it is no accident that
every one of these things has made its way later into a story of
mine.

*an art
and a craft
and a
marvelous
magic*

But memories themselves are not enough to create the
fusion that fires a story. To have read widely and deeply, to
have soaked oneself in the words and ideas of other writers,
to have seen what is possible and wonderful, to have listened
to the music of their words and to have read the work of the
masters must be a help for any writer discovering his own
technique, her own voice.

My own writing has taken all my years to develop—is
still developing, I hope—and it has happened in parallel
with my life and my reading. Once the spark is there—and
with me the spark is always the result of some fusion between
events I have lived or witnessed or discovered—then comes
the time for research, and with research a growing confidence
that I have the wherewithal to write it and then a conviction
that I have a burning need to write it.

But I must wait for the moment before I begin (procrasti-
nation has its uses!), until the story is ripe. This process can be
five minutes (unlikely) or five years. All I know is that you
can't hurry it. The story will be written when the moment is

right. I learned some time ago not to force the pace, not to dic-
tate the story but to allow the story time to find its own voice to
weave itself, to dream itself out in my head so that, by the time
I set pen to paper, I feel I am living inside that story. I must
know the places; I must know the people. I may still not
know exactly what will happen—and certainly not how it
might end. That often emerges through the writing. But I do
know by now the world of my story intimately, its tone and
tune, its cadence and rhythm. I feel I am living inside it, that
even as I am writing about it, I am not the creator of it at all,
but simply telling it as it happens, as I witness it. And when
it's written, I read it over, to hear the music of it in my head,
to be sure the tune and the story are in harmony. No note must
jar, or the dream of the story is interrupted.

The last and most important element in the alchemy that
produces this creative fusion is the sheer love of doing it, of
seeing if you can make magic from an empty page and a pen.
The truth is that it is not a trick. It is an art and a craft and
a marvelous magic, and I long with every
story to understand it better and to do it
better too.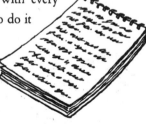

the giant's necklace

The necklace stretched from one end of the kitchen table to the
other, around the sugar bowl at the far end and back again, stopping only a few inches short of the toaster. The discovery on the
beach of a length of abandoned fishing line draped with seaweed
had first suggested the idea to Cherry, and every day of the vacation since then had been spent in one single-minded pursuit: the
creation of a necklace of glistening pink cowrie shells. She had
sworn to herself and to everyone else that the necklace would not
be complete until it reached the toaster, and when Cherry vowed
she would do something, she invariably did it.

Cherry was the youngest in a family of older brothers, four
of them, who had teased her relentlessly since the day she was
born, eleven years before. She referred to them as "the four mistakes," for it was a family joke that each son had been an attempt

to produce a daughter. To their huge delight, Cherry reacted passionately to any slight or insult whether intended or not. Their particular targets were her size, which was diminutive compared with theirs, her dark flashing eyes that could wither with one scornful look, but above all her ever-increasing femininity. Although the teasing was interminable it was rarely hurtful, nor was it intended to be, for her brothers adored her, and she knew it.

Cherry was poring over her necklace, still in her dressing gown. Breakfast had just been cleared away, and she was alone with her mother. She fingered the shells lightly, turning them gently until the entire necklace lay flat with the rounded pink of the shells all uppermost. Then she bent down and breathed on each of them in turn, polishing them carefully with a napkin.

"There's still the sea in them," she said to no one in particular. "You can still smell it, and I washed them and washed them, you know."

"You've only got today, Cherry," said her mother, coming over to the table and putting an arm around her. "Just today, that's all. We're off back home tomorrow morning first thing. Why don't you call it a day, dear? You've been at it every day— you *must* be tired of it by now. There's no need to go on, you know. We all think it's a fine necklace and quite long enough. It's long enough surely?"

Cherry shook her head slowly. "Nope," she said. "Only that little bit left to do and then it's finished."

"But they'll take hours to collect, dear," her mother said weakly, recognizing and at the same time respecting her daughter's persistence.

"Only a few hours," said Cherry, bending over, her brows furrowing critically as she inspected a flaw in one of her shells, "that's all it'll take. D'you know, there are five thousand, three hundred and twenty-five shells in my necklace already? I counted them, so I know."

"Isn't that enough, dear?" her mother said desperately.

"Nope," said Cherry. "I said I'd reach the toaster, and I'm going to reach the toaster."

Her mother turned away to continue drying the dishes.

"Well, I can't spend all day on the beach today, Cherry," she said. "If you haven't finished by the time we come away, I'll have to leave you there. We've got to pack up and tidy the house—there'll be no time in the morning."

"I'll be all right," said Cherry, cocking her head to one side to view the necklace from a different angle. "There's never been a necklace like this before, not in all the world. I'm sure there hasn't." And then: "You can leave me there, Mum, and I'll walk back. It's only a mile or so along the cliff path and half a mile back across the fields. I've done it before on my own. It's not far."

There was a thundering on the stairs and a sudden rude invasion of the kitchen. Cherry was surrounded by her four brothers, who leaned over the table in mock appreciation of her necklace.

"Ooh, pretty."

"Do they come in other colors? I mean, pink's not my color."

"Bit big though, isn't it?" said one of them—she didn't know which, and it didn't matter. He went on: "I mean it's a bit big for a necklace."

War had been declared again, and Cherry responded predictably.

"That depends," she said calmly, shrugging her shoulders because she knew that would irritate them.

"On what does it depend?" said her eldest brother pompously.

"On who's going to wear it of course, ninny," she said swiftly.

"Well, who is going to wear it?" he replied.

"It's for a giant," she said, her voice full of serious innocence. "It's a giant's necklace, and it's still not big enough."

It was the perfect answer, an answer she knew would send her brothers into fits of hysterical hilarity. She loved to make them laugh at her and could do it at the drop of a hat. Of course she no more believed in giants than they did, but if it tickled them pink to believe she did, then why not pretend?

She turned on them, fists flailing, and chased them back up the stairs, her eyes burning with simulated fury. "Just cos you don't believe in anything 'cept motorbikes and football and all that rubbish, just cos you're great big, fat, ignorant pigs . . ." She hurled insults up the stairs after them, and the worse the insults became the more they loved it.

Boat Cove just below Zennor Head was the beach they had found and occupied. Every year for as long as Cherry could remember, they had rented the same granite cottage, set back in the fields below the Eagle's Nest, and every year they came to the same beach because no one else did. In two weeks not another soul had ventured down the winding track through the bracken from the coastal path. It was a long climb down and a very much longer one up. The beach itself was almost hidden from the path that ran along the cliff top a hundred feet above. It was private and perfect and theirs. The boys swam in among the rocks, diving and snorkeling for hours on end. Her mother and father would sit side by side on striped deck chairs. She would read endlessly, and he would close his eyes against the sun and dream for hours on end.

Cherry moved away from them and clambered over the rocks to a narrow strip of sand in the cove beyond the rocks, and here it was that she mined for the cowrie shells. In the gritty sand under the cliff face she had found a particularly rich deposit, so they were not hard to find, but she was looking for pink cowrie shells of a uniform length, color, and shape—and that was what took the time. Occasionally the boys would swim around the rocks and into her little beach, emerging from the sea all goggled and flippered to mock her. But as she paid them little attention, they soon tired and went away again. She knew time was running short. This was her very last chance to find enough shells to com-plete the giant's necklace, and it had to be done.

The sea was calmer that day than she had ever seen it. The heat beat down from a windless, cloudless sky; even the gulls and kittiwakes seemed to be silenced by the sun. Cherry searched on, stopping only for a picnic lunch of pasties and tomatoes with the family before returning at once to her shells.

In the end the heat proved too much for her mother and father, who left the beach earlier than usual mid-afternoon to begin to tidy up the cottage. The boys soon followed because they had tired of finding miniature crabs and seaweed instead of the sunken wrecks and treasure they had been seeking, so that by teatime Cherry was left on her own on the beach with strict instructions to keep her hat on, not to swim alone, and to be back well before dark. She had calculated she needed one hundred and fifty more cowrie shells, and so far she had found only eighty. She would be back, she insisted, when she had finished collect-ing enough shells and not before.

Had she not been so immersed in her search, sifting the shells through her fingers, she would have noticed the dark gray bank of clouds rolling in from the Atlantic. She would have noticed the whitecaps gathering out at sea and the tide moving remorselessly in to cover the rocks between her and Boat Cove. When the clouds cut off the warmth from the sun as evening came on and the sea turned gray, she shivered with cold and slipped on her sweater and jeans. She did look up then and saw that the sea was angry, but she saw no threat in that and did not look back over her shoulder toward Boat Cove. She was aware that time was running short, so she went down on her knees again and dug feverishly in the sand. There were still thirty shells to collect, and she was not going home without them.

It was the baleful sound of a foghorn somewhere out at sea

beyond Gurnard's Head that at last forced Cherry to consider her own predicament. Only then did she take some account of the incoming tide. She looked for the rocks she would have to clamber over to reach Boat Cove again and the winding track that would take her up to the cliff path and safety, but they were gone. Where they should have been, the sea was already driving in against the cliff face. She was cut off. For many moments Cherry stared in disbelief and wondered if her memory was deceiving her, until the sea, sucked back into the Atlantic for a brief moment, revealed the rocks that marked her route back to Boat Cove. Then she realized at last that the sea had undergone a grim metamorphosis. In a confusion of wonder and fear she looked out to sea at the heaving ocean that moved in toward her, seeing it now as a writhing gray monster breathing its fury on the rocks with every pounding wave.

Still Cherry did not forget her shells, but wrapped them inside her towel and tucked them into her sweater and waded out through the surf toward the rocks. If she timed it right, she reasoned, she could scramble back over them and into the cove as the surf retreated. And she reached the first of the rocks without too much difficulty; the sea here seemed to be protected from the force of the ocean by the rocks farther out. Holding fast to the first rock she came to, and with the sea up around her waist, she waited for the next incoming wave to break and retreat. The wave was unexpectedly weak and fell limply on the rocks around her. She knew her moment had come and took it. She was not to know that piling up far out at sea was the first of the giant storm waves that had gathered several hundred miles out in the Atlantic, bringing with it all the momentum and violence of the deep ocean.

The rocks were slippery underfoot, and more than once Cherry slipped down into seething white rock pools where she had played so often when the tide was out. But she struggled on until finally she had climbed high enough to be able to see the thin strip of sand that was all that was left of Boat Cove. It was only a few yards away, so close. Until now she had been crying involuntarily, but now, as she recognized the little path up through the bracken, her heart was lifted with hope and anticipation. She knew that the worst was over, that if the sea would only hold back, she would reach the sanctuary of the cove. She turned and looked behind her to see how far away the next wave was, just to reassure herself that she had enough time. But the great surge of green water was on her before she could register either disappointment or fear. She was hurled back against the rock below her and covered at once by the sea. She was conscious as she went down that she was drowning, but she still clutched her shells against her chest and was glad she had enough of them at last to finish the giant's necklace. Those were her last thoughts before the sea took her away.

Cherry lay on her side where the tide had lifted her and coughed until her lungs were clear. She woke as the sea came in once again and frothed around her legs. She rolled over on her back, feeling the salt spray on her face, and saw that it was night. The sky above her was dashed with stars, and the moon rode through the clouds.

She scrambled to her feet, one hand still holding her precious shells close to her. Instinctively she backed away from the sea and looked around her. With growing dismay, she saw that she had been thrown back on the wrong side of the rocks, that she was not in Boat Cove. The tide had left only a few feet of sand and rock between her and the cliff face. There was no way back through the sea to safety.

She turned around to face the cliff that she realized would be her last hope, for she remembered that this little beach vanished completely at high tide. If she stayed where she was, she would surely be swept away again, and this time she might not be so fortunate. But the cold seemed to have calmed her, and she reasoned

more deliberately now, wondering why she had not tried climbing the cliff before. She had hurried into her first attempt at
escape, and it had very nearly cost her her life. She would wait
this time until the sea forced her up the cliff. Perhaps the tide
would not come in that far. Perhaps they would be looking for
her by now. It was dark. Surely they would be searching. Surely
they must find her soon. After all, they knew where she was. Yes,
she thought, best just to wait and hope.

She settled down on a ledge of rock that was the first step up
onto the cliff face, drew her knees up to her chin to keep out the
chill, and waited. She watched as the sea crept ever closer, each
wave lashing her with spray and eating away gradually at the
beach. She closed her eyes and prayed, hoping against hope that
when she opened them, the sea would be retreating. But her
prayers went unanswered, and the sea came in to cover the beach.
Once or twice she thought she heard voices above her on the cliff
path, but when she called out, no one came. She continued to
shout for help every few minutes, forgetting that it was futile
against the continuous roar and hiss of the waves. A pair of raucous white gulls flew down from the cliffs to investigate her, and
she called to them for help, but they did not seem to understand
and wheeled away into the night.

She stayed sitting on her rock until the waves threatened to dislodge her, and then reluctantly she began her climb. She would go as far as she needed to and no farther. She had scanned the first few feet above for footholds, and it did look quite a simple climb to begin with, and so it proved. But her hands were numb with cold, and her legs began to tremble with the strain almost at once. She could see that the ledge she had now reached was the last deep one visible on the cliff face. The shells in her jersey were restricting her freedom of movement, so she decided she would leave them there. Wrapped tight in the towel, they would be quite safe. She took the soaking bundle out of her jersey and placed it carefully against the rock face on the ledge beside her, pushing it in as far as it would go. "I'll be back for you," she said, and reached up for the next lip of rock. Just below her, the sea crashed against the cliff as if it wanted to suck her from the rock face and claim her once again. Cherry determined not to look down but to concentrate on the climb.

She imagined at first that the glow of light above her was from a flashlight, and she shouted and screamed until she was weak from the effort of it. But although no answering call came from the night, the light remained, a pale beckoning light whose source now seemed to her wider, perhaps, than that of a

The sea crashed against the cliff as if it wanted to suck her from the rock face.

flashlight. With renewed hope that had rekindled her strength and her courage, Cherry inched her way up the cliff toward the light until she found herself at the entrance to a narrow cave that was filled with a flickering yellow light like that of a candle shaken by the wind. She hauled herself up into the mouth of the cave and sat down, exhausted, looking back down at the furious sea frothing beneath her. Relief and joy surged within her, and she laughed aloud in triumph. She was safe, and she had defied the sea and won. Her one regret was that she had had to leave her cowrie shells behind on the ledge. They were high enough, she thought, to escape the sea. She would fetch them tomorrow after the tide had gone down again.

For the first time, she now began to think of her family and how worried they would be, but the thought of walking in through the front door all dripping and dramatic made her almost choke with excitement.

As she reached forward to brush a sharp stone from the sole of her foot, Cherry noticed that the narrow entrance to the cave was half sealed in. She ran her fingers over the stones and cement to make sure, for the light was poor. It was at that moment that she recognized exactly where she was. She recalled now the giant fledgling cuckoo one of her brothers had spotted being fed by a tiny rock pipit earlier in the vacation, how they had quarreled over the binoculars and how when she finally usurped them and made her escape across the rocks, she had found the cuckoo perched at the entrance to a narrow cave some way up the cliff face from the beach.

She had asked then about the man-made wall, and her father had told her of the old tin mines whose lodes and adits criss-crossed the entire coastal area around Zennor. This one, he said, might have been the mine they called Wheel North Grylls, and he thought the adit must have been walled up to prevent the seas from entering the mine in a storm. It was said there had been an accident in the mine only a few years after it was opened, over a hundred years before, and that the mine had had to close soon after when the mine owners ran out of money to make the neces-sary repairs. The entire story came back to her now, and she wondered where the cuckoo was and whether the rock pipit had died with the effort of keeping the fledgling alive. Tin mines, she thought, lead to the surface, and the way home. That thought and her natural inquisitiveness about the source of light per-suaded her to her feet and into the tunnel.

The adit became narrower and lower as she crept forward, so that she had to go down on her hands and knees and sometimes flat on her stomach. Although she was not out of the wind, it seemed colder. She felt she was moving downward for a minute or two, for the blood was coming to her head and her weight was heavy on her hands. Then, quite suddenly, she found the ground leveling out and saw a large tunnel ahead of her. There was no doubt as to which way she should turn, for one way the tunnel was black and the other way was lighted with candles that lined the lode wall as far as she could see. She called out, "Anyone there? Anyone there?" and paused to listen for the reply, but all she could hear was the muffled roar of the sea and the continuous echoing of dripping water.

The tunnel widened now, and she could walk upright again, but her feet hurt against the stone, so she moved slowly, feeling her way gently with each foot. She had gone only a short distance when she heard the tapping for the first time, distinct and rhythmic, a sound that was instantly recognizable as hammering. It became sharper and noticeably more metallic as she moved up the tunnel. She could hear the distant murmur of voices and the sound of falling stone. Even before she came out of the tunnel and into the vast cave, she knew she had happened upon a working mine.

The cave was dark in all but one corner, and here she could see two men bending to their work, their backs toward her. One of them was inspecting the rock face closely while the other swung his hammer with controlled power, pausing only to spit on his hands from time to time. They wore round hats with turned-up brims that served also as candlesticks, for a lighted candle was fixed to each, the light dancing with the shadows along the cave walls as they worked.

Cherry watched for some moments until she made up her mind what to do. She longed to rush up to them and tell of her escape and to ask them to take her to the surface, but a certain shyness overcame her and she held back. Her chance to interrupt came when they sat down against the rock face and opened their canteens. She was in the shadows, and they still could not see her.

"Tea looks cold again," one of them said gruffly. " 'Tis always cold. I'm sure she makes it wi' cold water."

"Oh, stop your moaning, Father," said the other—a younger voice, Cherry felt. "She does her best. She's five little ones to look after and precious little to do it on. She does her best. You mustn't keep on at her so. It upsets her. She does her best."

"So she does, lad, so she does. And so for that matter do I, but that don't stop her moaning at me and it'll not stop me moaning at her. If we didn't moan at each other, lad, we'd have precious little else to talk about, and that's a fact. She expects it of me, lad, and I expects it of her."

"Excuse me," Cherry said tentatively. She felt she had eaves-dropped for long enough. She approached them slowly. "Excuse me, but I've got a bit lost. I climbed the cliff, you see, cos I was cut off from the cove. I was trying to get back, but I couldn't, and I saw this light and so I climbed up. I want to get home, and I wondered if you could help me get to the top?"

"Top?" said the older one, peering into the dark. "Come closer, lad, where we can see you."

"She's not a lad, Father. Are you blind? Can you not see 'tis a filly. 'Tis a young filly, all wet through from the sea. Come," the young man said, standing up and beckoning Cherry in. "Don't be afeared, little girl; we shan't harm you. Come on, you can have some of my tea if you like."

They spoke their words in a manner Cherry had never heard before. It was not the usual Cornish burr, but heavier and rougher in tone and somehow old-fashioned. There were so many questions in her mind.

"But I thought the mine was closed a hundred years ago," she said nervously. "That's what I was told, anyway."

"Well, you was told wrong," said the old man, whom Cherry

could see more clearly now under his candle. His eyes were white and set far back in his head—unnaturally so, she thought—and his lips and mouth seemed a vivid red in the candlelight.

"Closed, closed indeed; does it look closed to you? D'you think we're digging for worms? Over four thousand tons of tin last year and nine thousand of copper ore, and you ask is the mine closed? Over twenty fathoms below the sea this mine goes. We'll dig right out under the ocean, most of the way to 'Merica, afore we close down this mine."

He spoke passionately now, almost angrily, so that Cherry felt she had offended him.

"Hush, Father," said the young man, taking off his jacket and wrapping it around Cherry's shoulders. "She doesn't want to hear all about that. She's cold and wet. Can't you see? Now, let's make a little fire to warm her through. She's shivered right through to her bones. You can see she is."

"They all are," said the old tinner, pulling himself to his feet. "They all are." And he shuffled past her into the dark. "I'll fetch the wood," he muttered, and then added, "for all the good it'll do."

"What does he mean?" Cherry asked the young man, for whom she felt an instant liking. "What did he mean by that?"

"Oh, pay him no heed, little girl," he said. "He's an old man now and tired of the mine. We're both tired of it, but we're proud of it, see, and we've nowhere else to go, nothing else to do."

He had a kind voice that was reassuring to Cherry. He seemed somehow to know the questions she wanted to ask, for he answered them now without her asking.

"Sit down by me while you listen, girl," he said. "Father will make a fire to warm you, and I shall tell you how we come to be here. You won't be afeared now, will you?"

Cherry looked up into his face, which was younger than she had expected from his voice, but like his father's, the eyes seemed sad and deep-set, yet they smiled at her gently and she smiled back.

"That's my girl. It was a new mine this, promising, everyone said. The best tin in Cornwall, and that means the best tin in the world. Eighteen sixty-five it started up, and they were looking for tinners, and so Father found a cottage down by Treveal and came to work here. I was already fourteen, so I joined him down in the mine. We prospered and the mine prospered, to start with. Mother and the little children had full bellies, and there was talk of sinking a fresh shaft. Times were good and promised to be better."

Cherry sat transfixed as the story of the disaster unfolded. She heard how they had been trapped by a fall of rock, about how they had worked to pull them away, but behind every rock was another rock and another rock. She heard how they had never even heard any sound of rescue. They had died, he said, in two days or so because the air was bad and because there was too little of it.

"Father has never accepted it; he still thinks he's alive, that he goes home to Mother and the little children each evening. But he's dead, just like me. I can't tell him, though, for he'd not understand and it would break his heart if he ever knew."

"So you aren't real," said Cherry, trying to grasp the implications of his story. "So I'm just imagining all this. You're just a dream."

"No dream, my girl," said the young man, laughing out loud. "No more'n we're imagining you. We're real right enough, but we're dead and have been for a hundred years and more. Ghosts, spirits, that's what living folk call us. Come to think of it, that's what I called us when I was alive."

Cherry was on her feet suddenly and backing away.

"No need to be afeared, little girl," said the young man, holding out his hand toward her. "We won't harm you. No one can harm you, not now. Look, he's started the fire already. Come over and warm yourself. Come, it'll be all right, girl. We'll look after you. We'll help you."

"But I want to go home," Cherry said, feeling the panic rising in her voice and trying to control it. "I know you're kind, but I want to go home. My mother will be worried about me. They'll be out looking for me. Your light saved my life, and I want to thank you. But I must go or else they'll worry themselves sick; I know they will."

"You going back home?" the young man asked, and then he nodded. "I s'pose you'll want to see your family again."

"Course I am," said Cherry, perplexed by the question. "Course I do."

"'Tis a pity," he said sadly. "Everyone passes through and no one stays. They all want to go home, but then so do I. You'll want me to guide you to the surface, I s'pose."

"I'm not the first then?" Cherry said. "There's been others climb up into the mine to escape from the sea? You've saved lots of people."

"A few," said the tinner, nodding. "A few."

"You're a kind person," Cherry said, warming to the sadness in the young man's voice. "I never thought ghosts would be kind."

singing for mrs. pettigrew

"We're just people, people who've passed on," replied the young man, taking her elbow and leading her toward the fire. "There's nice people and there's nasty people. It's the same if you're alive or if you're dead. You're a nice person; I can tell that, even though I haven't known you for long. I'm sad because I should like to be alive again with my friends and go rabbiting or blackberrying up by the chapel near Treveal like I used to. The sun always seemed to be shining then. After it happened, I used to go up to the surface often and move among the people in the village. I went to see my family, but if I spoke to them, they never seemed to hear me, and of course they can't see you. You can see them, but they can't see you. That's the worst of it. So I don't go up much now, just to collect wood for the fire and a bit of food now and then. I stay down here with Father in the mine and we work away day after day, and from time to time someone like you comes up the tunnel from the sea and lightens our darkness. I shall be sad when you go."

The old man was hunched over the fire, rubbing his hands and holding them out over the heat.

"Not often we have a fire," he said, his voice more sprightly now. "Only on special occasions. Birthdays, of course, we always have a fire on birthdays back at the cottage. Martha's next. You don't know her; she's my only daughter—she'll be eight on September tenth. She's been poorly, you know—her lungs, that's what the doctor said." He sighed deeply. "'Tis dreadful damp in the cottage. 'Tis well nigh impossible to keep it out." There was a tremor in the old man's voice that betrayed his emotion. He looked up at Cherry, and she could see the tears in his eyes. "She looks a bit like you, my dear, raven-haired and as pretty as a picture, but not so tall, not so tall. Come in closer, my dear; you'll be warmer that way."

Cherry sat with them by the fire till it died away to nothing. She longed to go, to get home among the living, but the old man talked on of his family and their little one-room cottage with a ladder to the bedroom, where they all huddled together for warmth, of his friends that used to meet in the Tinners' Arms every evening. There were tales of wrecking and smuggling, and all the while the young man sat silent until there was a lull in the story.

"Father," he said. "I think our little friend would like to go home now. Shall I take her up as I usually do?"

The old man nodded and waved his hand in dismissal. "Come back and see us sometime, if you've a mind to," he said, and then put his face in his hands.

"Good-bye," said Cherry. "Thank you for the fire and for helping me. I won't forget you."

But the old man didn't reply.

The journey through the mine was long and difficult. She held fast to the young tinner's waist as they walked silently through the dark tunnels, stopping every now and then to climb a ladder to the lode above until finally they could look up the shaft above them and see the daylight.

"It's dawn," said the young man, looking up.

"I'll be back in time for breakfast," said Cherry, setting her foot on the ladder.

"You'll remember me?" the young tinner asked, and Cherry nodded, unable to speak. She felt a strange affinity with him and his father. "And if you should ever need me, come back again. You may need me, and I shall be here. I go nowhere else."

"Thank you," said Cherry. "I won't forget. I doubt anyone is going to believe me when I tell them about you. No one believes in ghosts, not up there."

"I doubt it, too. Be happy, little friend," he said. And he was gone, back into the tunnel. Cherry waited until the light from the candle in his hat had vanished, then turned eagerly to the ladder and began to climb up toward the light.

She found herself in a place she knew well, high on the moor by Zennor Quoit. She stood by the ruined mine workings and looked down at the sleeping village shrouded in mist, and the calm blue sea beyond. The storm had passed, and there was scarcely a breath of wind even on the moor. It was only ten minutes' walk down through the bracken, across the road by the Eagle's Nest, and down the farm track to the cottage, where her family would be waiting. She began to run, but her clothes were still heavy and wet, and she was soon reduced to a fast walk. All the while she was determining where she would begin her story, wondering how much they would believe. At the top of the lane, she stopped to consider how best to make her entrance. Should she ring the bell and be found standing there, or should she just walk in and surprise them there at breakfast? She longed to see the joy on their faces, to feel the warmth of their arms around her, and to bask once again in their affection.

She saw as she came around the corner by the cottage that there was a long blue Land Rover parked in the lane, bristling with antennae. *Coastguard* she read on the side. As she came down the steps, she noticed that the back door of the cottage was open and she could hear voices inside. She stole in on tiptoe. The kitchen was full of uniformed men drinking tea, and around the table sat her family, dejection and despair etched on every face. They hadn't seen her yet. One of the uniformed men had put down his cup and was speaking. His voice was low and hushed.

"You're sure the towel is hers. No doubts about it?"

Cherry's mother shook her head.

"It's her towel," she said quietly, "and they are her shells. She must have put them up there, must have been the last thing she did."

Cherry saw her shells spread out on the open towel and stifled a shout of joy.

"We have to say," he went on. "We have to say then, most regrettably, that the chances of finding your daughter alive now are very slim. It seems she must have tried to climb the cliff to escape the heavy seas and fallen in. We've scoured the cliff top for miles in both directions and covered the entire beach, and there's no sign of her. She must have been washed out to sea. We must conclude that she is missing, and we have to presume that she drowned."

Cherry could listen no longer but burst into the room, shouting.

"I'm home; I'm home. Look at me; I'm not drowned at all. I'm here! I'm home!"

The tears were running down her face.

But no one in the room even turned to look in her direction. Her brothers cried openly, one of them clutching the giant's necklace.

"But it's me," she shouted again. "Me, can't you see? It's me and I've come back. I'm all right. Look at me."

But no one did, and no one heard.

The giant's necklace lay spread out on the table.

"So she'll never finish it after all," said her mother softly. "Poor Cherry. Poor dear Cherry."

And in that one moment Cherry knew and understood that she was right, that she would never finish her necklace, that she belonged no longer with the living but had passed on beyond. ✢

we are what we read

The English poet Edward Thomas once wrote that as a young boy he preferred birds to books. Me, too, though being a little savage, I preferred bird nesting to bird-watching. I collected eggs and butterflies and Turf cigarette footballer cards, where all the footballers had big heads. I played rugby and cricket and conkers and jacks and marbles. I did read, but only when I had to, and then it was mostly *Eagle* or Enid Blyton, probably because both were banned at home. By rights, by all logic, I should have grown up an avid reader. Our house groaned with books. They lined the walls in every room, even the bathroom. I had a grandfather called Émile Cammaerts, an eminent bilingual poet and philosopher, who had his poetry set to music by Edward Elgar; and a stepfather, Jack Morpurgo, who was both a publisher and a writer. Both were intellectuals, both bookmen to the core. This pedigree should have helped—it didn't. It probably hindered—but that's not their fault.

I may not have liked books, but I did like stories. I simply loved stories. And now, these many years later, I know why. I think I also know how it was that later on my love of stories turned into a dislike of books, even a fear of them. My mother

was an actor (actress in those days) and a good one, too—
Royal Academy of Dramatic Art. Stratford-upon-Avon,
and all that. When I was very little, she'd come and sit on my
bed and read me a story, or a poem or two. I don't remember
any pictures in these books. The pictures came into my head
with the words she spoke, words that sounded to me like
familiar music. I treasured, then and now, those precious
moments alone with my mother, the only time we were truly
alone in a busy household. And it was the story that bound
us, the story and the tune of the words. The book was the living link between us. Every bedtime I dreaded the coming of
the end, the finality of the last line of the poem or story.

    She read me Aesop's fables, Masefield and de la Mare
and Belloc and Longfellow and Kipling and Edward Lear's
"The Jumblies," a great favorite of hers and mine:

> They went to sea in a Sieve, they did,
>
>   In a Sieve they went to sea:
>
> In spite of all their friends could say,
>
> On a winter's morn, on a stormy day,
>
>   In a Sieve they went to sea!
>
> And when the Sieve turned round and round,
>
> And every one cried, "You'll all be drowned!"
>
> They called aloud, "Our Sieve ain't big,
>
> But we don't care a button! we don't care a fig!
>
>   In a Sieve we'll go to sea!"
>
>   Far and few, far and few,

Are the lands where the Jumblies live;

Their heads are green, and their hands are blue,

And they went to sea in a Sieve.

Story time over, she'd leave me in the darkness with just the smell of her face powder. The door would be left open a chink, because she knew I liked it that way. Soon enough, though, it would be closed completely—because "boys your age shouldn't be afraid of the dark." In the terrifying, impene⁄ trable blackness, the blackness of death I thought it was, I would try all I could to relive the story, remember the poem. Stories and poems, and the singing words that made them, lightened my darkness, were a joy and a comfort to me all through my early childhood.

Then, at five or six, "unwillingly to school" I went, trudg⁄ ing the leafy pavement through the pea⁄soup smogs to St. Matthias Primary School on the Warwick Road, and later, even more unwillingly, to boarding school in Sussex. In both places, words and books became a threat. They were no longer magical, and certainly not musical. Words were to be spelled, forming sentences and clauses, with punctuation, with neat handwriting and without blotches. Some words were called nouns or pronouns or verbs. Some words were to be recited standing up, my memory stifled and numbed by terror, my tongue and throat cramped with a stutter. There were dictations, copying, précis, and comprehensions, and all were tested and marked. A few red ticks, very few. But more often a multitude of red crosses and red slashes covered my exercise books like bleeding cuts. Then there were the pun⁄ ishments. Misspelled words had to be written out fifty—a hundred—times. For any untidiness there was detention and more lines to be written out. And often, for persistent under-achieving, to encourage us to do better, there was the dreaded visit to the headmaster's study for the cane. Worst of all, though, was the disapproval at home for a bad report, official confirmation of my failures and failings. "If you want to pass your exams, you'll have to read more," I was told. So I was given *Oliver Twist* to read—I think I was eight at the time.

Stories and poems had taken on an entirely different hue. The music had died; the magic, the joy, and the comfort were gone. I was no longer read to in bed, because I wasn't at home much, and when I was, I was thought to be too old by now. Books became a source of dread for me, a reminder of my own failure to achieve. So I went bird nesting instead of reading. You can blame the scarcity of mistle thrushes in Sussex today on *Oliver Twist.* Like most children, I wanted very much to succeed at something. I could play cricket really well, took to it easily; became brilliant at rugby; utterly amaz-ing at marbles; and a veritable genius at jacks.

Somehow, though, through all this, I must have read just enough to keep the memory of the music alive: schoolboy stories, derring-do, adventures in comic or word form. G. A. Henty I remember well, *With Lee in Virginia, With Clive in India;* C. S. Forester, too—all the Hornblower stories. I did become truly passionate about one book, a book I read again and again, so strongly did I identify with its hero. I was Jim Hawkins in *Treasure Island.* I lived it with him: hid in the bar-rel of apples on board the *Hispaniola,* overheard the horrible conspiracy, witnessed murder and skulduggery, fought the baddies alongside the goodies, sailed a ship all on my own. Stevenson modeled Jim Hawkins on me—no question. All these years later, he's still the writer I most admire and most long to be. But back in class, back at home, too, books simply made me feel frightened and inadequate. I lied my way out of trouble in both places, read Classics Illustrated (comic-book versions of the real thing) and claimed I had read *A Tale of Two Cities* and *War and Peace* and *Jane Eyre.* They had pictures, and they had cracking stories. Most serious books remained closed books for me for a long while yet.

I did, just once, briefly discover that early love of words my mother had instilled in me. I was taken to see Paul Scofield playing Hamlet at the Phoenix Theatre, in the mid-fifties it must have been. I would have been about twelve. I listened entranced, enchanted, to the concerto of poetry he was playing that night. I have never forgotten it. And I did have one teacher, just one, Sidney Sopwith, who tried to encourage me to believe I had a brain in my head, that there was more to life than rugby, and that one day I'd find that out for myself. But by now I was typecast as a good chap and a bit of a dummy and, sadly, was quite happy enough and lazy enough to play that role.

After a brief period in the army, I went to university and studied English and French and philosophy. I just about muddled through, still burdened by that same deep sense of inadequacy whenever I opened a book or tried to write an essay. But then, in my third year at King's College London, I happened to read *Sir Gawain and the Green Knight* and LOVED it. I was riveted by the pace of the story, the richness of the language, and for the first time in a very long while found a place for myself inside a work of poetry or fiction. Suddenly I wasn't an outsider. I was Gawain, just as I had been Jim Hawkins. I heard the music in the words again, was a child again, was a reader again.

Years later I wrote a story about just such a child, a reluctant reader you might call him, inspired one day by someone who loves stories, who through the power of her storytelling and her passion for books changes the child's life. I called it "I Believe in Unicorns." Like many of my stories, it has appeared in several forms. I love that, the transformation into a film, into an opera, into a stage play; each breathes new life, a different life, into a story. In this case this short story was developed into a novella, given greater depth and space within which to live. But what follows here is the original, the essence of the story, if you like.

i believe in unicorns

My name is Tomas Porec. I was seven years old when I first met the unicorn lady. I believed in unicorns then. I am nearly twenty now, and because of her I still believe in unicorns.

My little town, hidden deep in its own valley, was an ordinary place, pretty enough but ordinary. I know that now. But when I was seven, it was a place of magic and wonder to me. It was my place, my home. I knew every cobbled alleyway, every lamppost in every street. I fished in the stream below the church, tobogganed the slopes in winter, swam in the lake in the summer. On Sundays my mother and father would take me on walks or on picnics, and I'd roll down the hills, over and over, and end up lying there on my back, giddy with joy, the world spinning above me.

I never did like school, though. It wasn't the school's fault, nor the teachers'. I just wanted to be outside all the time. I longed always to be running free up in the hills. As soon as school was over, it was back home for some bread and honey—my father kept his own bees on the hillside—then out to play. But one afternoon my mother had other ideas. She had to do some shopping in town, she said, and wanted me to go with her.

"I hate shopping," I told her.

"I know that, dear," she said. "That's why I'm taking you to the library. It'll be interesting. Something different. You can listen to stories for an hour or so. It'll be good for you. There's a new librarian lady, and she tells stories after school to any children who want to listen. Everyone says she's wonderful."

"But I don't want to listen," I protested.

My mother simply ignored all my pleas, took me firmly by the hand, and led me to the town square. She walked me up the steps into the library. "Be good," she said, and she was gone.

I could see there was an excited huddle of children gathered in one corner. Some of them were from my school, but they all looked a lot younger than me. Some of them were infants! I certainly did not want to be with them. I was just about to turn and walk away in disgust when I noticed they were all jostling each other, as if they were desperate to get a better look at some-thing. Since I couldn't see what it was, I went a little closer. Suddenly, they were all sitting down and hushed, and there in the corner I saw a unicorn. He was lying absolutely still, his feet tucked neatly under him. I could see now that he was made of carved wood and painted white, but he was so lifelike that if he'd stood up and trotted off, I wouldn't have been at all sur-prised.

Beside the unicorn and just as motionless, just as neat, stood a lady with a smiling face, a bright, flowery scarf around her shoulders. When her eyes found mine, her smile beckoned me to join them. Moments later I found myself sitting on the floor with the others, watching and waiting. When she sat down slowly on the unicorn and folded her hands in her lap, I could feel expecta-tion all around me.

"The unicorn story!" cried a little girl. "Tell us the unicorn story. Please."

The lady talked so softly that I had to lean forward to hear her. But I wanted to hear her, everyone did, because every word she spoke was meant and felt, and sounded true. The story was about how the last two magic unicorns alive on earth had arrived just too late to get on Noah's ark with all the other animals. So they were left stranded on a mountaintop in the driving rain, watch- ing the ark sail away over the great flood into the distance. The waters rose and rose around them until their hooves were cov- ered, then their legs, then their backs, and so they had to swim. They swam and they swam—for hours, for days, for weeks, for years. They swam for so long, they swam so far, that in the end they turned into whales. This way they could swim easily. This way they could dive down to the bottom of the sea. But they never lost their magical powers and they still kept their wonderful horns, which is why there are to this day whales with unicorn's horns. They're called narwhals. And sometimes, when they've had enough of the sea and want to see children again, they swim up onto the beaches and find their legs and become unicorns again, magical unicorns.

After she had finished, no one spoke. It was as if we were all waking up from some dream we didn't want to leave. There were more stories, and poems, too. Some she read from books; some she made up herself or knew by heart.

Then a hand went up. It was a small boy from my school, Milos with the sticky-up hair. "Can I tell a story, miss?" he asked.

So, sitting on the unicorn, he told us his story. One after another after that, they wanted their turn on the magical unicorn. I longed to have a go myself, but I didn't dare. I was frightened of making a fool of myself, I think.

The hour flew by.

"What was it like?" my mother asked me on the way home.

"All right, I suppose," I told her. But at school the next day, I told all my friends what it was really like, all about the unicorn lady—everyone called her that—and her amazing stories and the fantastic magical storytelling power of the unicorn.

They came along with me to the library that afternoon. Day after day as word spread, the little group in the corner grew until there was a whole crowd of us. We would rush to the library now to get there first, to find a place close to the unicorn, close to the unicorn lady. Every story she told us held us entranced. She never told us to sit still. She didn't have to. Each day I wanted so much to sit on the unicorn and tell a story, but still I could never quite summon up the courage.

One afternoon the unicorn lady took out from her bag a rather old and damaged-looking book, all charred at the edges. It was, she told us, her very own copy of *The Little Match Girl,* by

Sitting on the magic unicorn, I heard my voice strong and loud.

Hans Christian Andersen. I was sitting that day very close to the unicorn lady's feet, looking up at the book. "Has it been burned?" I asked her.

"This is the most precious book I have, Tomas," she said. "I'll tell you why. When I was very little, I lived in another country. There were wicked people in my town who were frightened of the magic of stories and of the power of books, because stories make you think and dream; books make you want to ask questions. And they didn't want that. I was there with my father, watching them burn a great pile of books, when suddenly my father ran forward and plucked a book out of the fire. The soldiers beat him with sticks, but he held on to the book and wouldn't let go of it. It was this book. It's my favorite book in all the world. Tomas, would you like to come and sit on the unicorn and read it to us?"

I had never been any good at reading out loud. I would always stutter over my consonants, worry over long words. But now, sitting on the magic unicorn, I heard my voice strong and loud. It was like singing a song. The words danced on the air and everyone listened. That same day I took home my first book from the library, *Aesop's Fables,* because the unicorn lady had read them to us and I'd loved them. I read them aloud to my mother that night, the first time I'd ever read to her, and I could see she was amazed. I loved amazing my mother.

Then one summer morning, early, war came to our valley and shattered our lives. Before that morning I knew little of war. I knew some of the men had gone to fight, but I wasn't sure why. I had seen on television tanks shooting at houses and soldiers with guns running through the trees, but my mother always told me it was far away and I wasn't to worry.

I remember the moment. I was outside. My mother had sent me out to open up the hens and feed them, when I looked up and saw a single plane come flying in low over the town. I watched as it circled once and came again. That was when the bombs began to fall, far away at first, then closer, closer. We were all running then, running up into the woods. I was too frightened to cry. My father cried. I'd never seen him cry before, but it was from anger as much as fear.

Hidden high in the woods we could see the tanks and the soldiers all over the town, blasting and shooting as they went. A few hours later, after they had gone, we could hardly see the town anymore for the smoke. We waited until we were sure they had all gone, and then we ran back home. We were luckier than many.

Our house had not been damaged. It was soon obvious that the center of town had been hardest hit. Everyone seemed to be making their way there. I ran on ahead, hoping and praying that the library had not been bombed, that the unicorn lady and the unicorn were safe.

As I came into the square, I saw smoke rising from the roof of the library and flames licking out of the upper windows. We all saw the unicorn lady at the same moment. She was coming out of the library carrying the unicorn, staggering under its weight. I ran up the steps to help her. She smiled me her thanks as I took my share of the weight. Her eyes were red from the smoke. Between us we set the unicorn down at the foot of the steps, and she sat down, exhausted, racked with a fit of coughing. My mother fetched her a glass of water. It must have helped, because the coughing stopped, and all at once she was up on her feet, leaning on my shoulder for support.

"The books," she breathed. "The books."

When she began to walk back up the steps, I followed her without thinking.

"No, Tomas," she said. "You stay here and look after the unicorn." Then she was running up the steps into the library, only to reappear moments later, her arms piled high with books. That was the moment the rescue began. People seemed suddenly to surge past me up the steps and into the library, my mother and father among them.

It wasn't long before a whole system was set up. We children made two chains across the square from the library to the café opposite, and the books everyone rescued went from hand to hand, ending up in stacks on the floor of the café. The fire was burning ever more fiercely, the flames crackling, smoke billowing now from the roof. No fire engines came—we found out later that the fire station had been hit. Still the books came out. Still the fire burned and more and more people came to help, until the café was filled with books and we had to use the grocer's shop next door.

The moment came when there were suddenly no more books to pass along and we all wondered why. Then we saw everyone coming out of the library, and last of all the unicorn lady, helped by my father. They came slowly down the steps together, their faces smudged and blackened. The unicorn lady sat down heavily on the unicorn and looked up at the burning building. We children all gathered around her as if waiting for a story.

"We did it, children," she said. "We saved all we could, didn't we? I'm sitting on the unicorn, so any story I tell is true because we believe it can be true. We shall build our library up again just as it was. Meanwhile we shall look after the books. Every family can take home all the books they can manage and care for them. And when in one year or two or three we have our new library, then we shall all bring back our books, and we shall carry the magic unicorn inside and we shall all tell our stories again. All we have to do is make this story come true."

So it happened, just as the unicorn lady said it would. Like so many families in the town, we took home a wheelbarrow full of books and looked after them. Sure enough the library was rebuilt just the same as the old one, only by now everyone called it the Unicorn, and we all brought our books back just as the unicorn lady had told it in her story.

The day the library opened, because I had helped carry the unicorn out, I got to carry him back up the steps with the unicorn lady, and the whole town was there cheering and clapping, the flags flying, the band playing. It was the proudest and happiest day of my life.

Now, all these years later, we have peace in our valley. The unicorn lady is still the town librarian, still reading her stories to the children after school. As for me, I'm a writer now, a weaver of tales. And if from time to time I lose the thread of my story, all I have to do is go and sit on the magic unicorn and my story flows again. So believe me, I believe in unicorns. I believe in them absolutely. ✢

we are what we write

It was, thinking back, a remark-ably quick transition from the rediscovery of my love of words, of reading, of stories, of poems, to discovering I had a voice of my own, a storytell-ing voice, a writer's voice. I became a father first and then a teacher. Both helped in this discovery. I read to my own children at bedtime—although not often enough, my wife, Clare, tells me, and she's right, of course.

Sometimes, as fathers and mothers do, I made up stories I thought they'd like. And they did, too, sometimes. By day I was in my classroom trying to motivate children to want to read. I found the best way to do that was to read stories to them, to tell them tales. I suppose I was trying at home and at school to do what my mother had done for me all those years before, because I knew now how important that had been for me. But I was no actor. There was only one way, I discovered, to convince my audience of children, and that was to be con-vinced myself, utterly convinced, by everything I was reading or telling them. I had to mean it, not to fake it. And I found it was easier to mean it if I made it up myself and told it. There wasn't a book between us then, separating us.

I found common ground between me and many—I should say most—of the children I was now teaching. Many had already experienced difficulty in learning to read and write, as I had; had been bored by ill-chosen stories, often read to them by teachers who didn't much like stories or poems themselves; had for too long suffered the tyranny of punctuation tests and spelling tests and comprehension tests; were already deeply alienated from literature and simply not interested in anything a book had to offer. I had been there. I knew that before they could engage with stories (and certainly with literacy), all the fear and the resentment had to be excised. I would simply tell stories or read them, trying to make every one of them as enjoyable and compelling as I could, and I would not ask questions afterward, nor use the test to teach. Let them enjoy the stories, I thought. Then they might see and understand the need for punctuation and spelling. It might all begin to make some sense to them. Words would hold less fear for them; in fact, they might see that words could turn out to be fun and fascinating and filled with music and magic. And it worked; it really worked.

Of course, not all my children became instant book lovers, but some did, and that encouraged me to go one step further and see if I could make writers of them as well as readers. Now that they were beginning to enjoy words, to feel more at ease and at home with them, maybe, I thought, they could use words on paper and express how they felt, could experiment, paint pictures with words, make music with words, play with words. Maybe they could use their lives and their dreams and make their own stories and poems happen. Maybe they, too, could be writers.

At the time there were the most extraordinarily creative programs on BBC School Radio—*Living Language* and *Listening and Writing*. On one of those programs, I heard Ted Hughes's *Poetry in the Making*. For me, certainly, and for many

of the children I was teaching, it was a life-changing program. Here was one of our greatest poets saying: "Here's how
I do it; you can do it, too. Anyone can. You just drink in the
world around you. Look, feel, dream, read—and then tell it
your own way. And when you write, listen hard and you can
hear the music in the words, aloud in your head. Make music
and meaning merge. And it must matter. You have to care."

Fired up with new enthusiasm and confidence, my class
and I became poets and storytellers together, faced the same
blank page together. As they became readers and writers, so
did I. I was reading everything now: poetry, history, short
stories—I loved Hans Christian Andersen, Paul Gallico,
Jean Giono, Guy de Maupassant, Robert Louis Stevenson.
The children had their poems broadcast on BBC School
Radio—they were that good—and I published my first
book, more a pamphlet really. I called it *Children's Words,* an
anthology of writing by children (among them, one by a
young poet named Daniel Day-Lewis, age thirteen). With all
these young writers, I was discovering, and the children were
discovering, just how right Ted Hughes had been. We really
do have it in us to be writers, to be storytellers; we have only to
find our voices.

All this time, although I really wasn't aware of it then, I
was taking my own first tentative steps as a writer. I had
already tested myself as a storyteller—thirty-five expectant
children for half an hour's story time at the end of each school
day had done that. Confidence was growing. But I still had
not grasped that I could do more than entertain, and I knew
that entertaining was not enough for me. I knew that the best
books I had read, the best poems, had made me think and
wonder and question. But at the time I thought that it was

69

only geniuses that wrote such books, clever people, literary people. I was still encumbered, I suppose, by this feeling of intellectual and creative inadequacy. The stories I wrote, which were now being published, were thin, too contrived, never really getting to the heart of the matter. I wasn't sure I had it in me to do any better. It was an uncomfortable reality to confront. I almost gave up.

But then I got lucky. My life as a teacher was suddenly and dramatically altered. At my wife, Clare's, behest we upped sticks from Kent and moved down to deepest Devon. Both of us, as teachers, had felt that children could never learn enough within the confines of the classroom, that children—and city children in particular—would benefit hugely from the experience of living for a while in the countryside and working on a farm, as indeed Clare had done when she was little. Happily, she had the wherewithal financially to buy the large house and the farm we needed to set up an educational charity, Farms for City Children (FFCC), and off we went on our great adventure down to Devon, to Iddesleigh, to get it started. (It was rather like beginning a new novel, a moment of great hope and determination, and behind it all a rush of madness to the head!)

I will not write too much here about the thirty-plus years since, only to say that FFCC now has several farms: Nethercott in Devon, Wick Court in Gloucestershire, and Treginnis in Wales; there's one, too, in Vermont in America. Some sixty thousand children have come to the farms, harvesting, mucking out, feeding sheep and pigs and calves, and have had the week of their young lives and have gone home enriched, encouraged, and invigorated.

But quite unexpectedly, it turned out that I was the one

who benefited most from all this, for in moving to Devon, in immersing myself in farming, in working with the children and the farmers who were our partners in the project, in living with my family in a small tight-knit community, I inadvertently enriched myself hugely as a person, and so as a writer. I grew up. When I wrote now, I really had something I knew about, something I wanted to say, indeed needed to say. I came to know a place and its people, became fascinated with their history and their lives. Now I was beginning to write about what I cared about, not simply to entertain children or anyone else for that matter. I was exploring in my stories, my own hopes and doubts and fears, engaging with my own past and present. I was finding my voice.

So I would be out on the farm with the children, listening to them, to their stories, watching how they interacted with the animals, with one another. We would walk the fields and lanes, see and wonder at buzzards wheeling and mewing above us in the summer, watch larks rising off the hills and disappearing into the sky. We would stomp the muddy fields in winter, ford rushing streams to feed the lambing sheep. We would be there at births, at deaths. We would follow badger tracks through hedges, discover their droppings, glimpse deer and foxes and otters (Henry Williamson, the great author of *Tarka the Otter,* had been there on the banks of the same river before me); we'd see salmon and sea trout rise in the river and stay to watch a heron fishing. I would come back home afterward and dream up my stories around this place I had discovered with the children, a place I was coming to know and love, just as Edward Thomas knew and loved the woods and hangers above Steep in Hampshire. Now I was beginning to discover what Ted Hughes really meant in his *Poetry in the Making.* First immerse yourself in the world about you, become part of it; then you'll be able to write. It was from this total immersion that I was finding at last I had a story of my own to tell and a voice of my own with which to tell it.

Then one evening, Ted Hughes was there (this great poet) fishing on our river, and we met. He became a friend to us and to Farms for City Children, and he became my mentor as a writer. And just down the lane lived another great poet and great friend, Sean Rafferty, sadly still largely unknown, but the best-read man I have ever met. We all three of us exchanged ideas, gave one another poems and books on birthdays and Christmases, celebrated our publications, moaned about publishers. I was, of course, always the youngest and least distinguished, but I loved hearing them speak. Theirs were the feet I sat at, usually in front of a roaring fire, all of us with a glass of Bordeaux. It was a glowing time. And my books flowed: *War Horse, Waiting for Anya, King of the Cloud Forests, The White Horse of Zennor, All Around the Year* with Ted Hughes himself; and all the while the truth about them as writers, and about me, too, was becoming clear.

Don't pretend. Tell your tale. Speak with your own voice. We are what we write, I think, even more than we are what we read. ——

my one and only great escape

I still think of the house on the Essex coast where I grew up as my childhood home. But, in fact, it was my home for just four months of every year. The rest of the time I spent at my boarding school a whole world away, deep in the Sussex countryside. In my home by the sea they called me Michael. In my boarding school I was Morpurgo (or Pongo to my friends), and I became another person. I had two distinctively different lives, and so, in order to survive both, I had to become two very different people. Three times a year I had to make the changeover from home boy to schoolboy. Going back to school was always an agony of misery, a wretched ritual, a ritual I endured simply because I had to.

Then one evening at the beginning of the autumn term of 1953, I made up my mind that I would not endure it any longer, that I would run away, that I would not stay at my school and be

Morpurgo or Pongo anymore. I simply wanted to go home where I belonged and be Michael forever.

The agony began, as it always began, about ten days before the end of the holidays—in this case, the summer holidays. For eight blessed weeks I had been at home. We lived in a large and rambling old house in the center of a village called Bradwell-Juxta-Mare (near the sea). The house was called New Hall—*new* being mostly seventeenth century, with lots of beams and red bricks. It had a handsome Georgian front, with great sash windows, and one or two windows that weren't real windows at all but painted on—to save the window tax, I was told. House and garden lay hidden and protected behind a big brick wall.

Cycling out of the gate, as I often did, I turned left onto the village street toward Bradwell Quay and the sea, right toward the church, and the American air base, and then out over the marshes toward the ancient Saxon chapel of Saint Peter's near the seawall itself. Climb the seawall and there was the great brown, soupy North Sea and always a wild, wet wind blowing. I felt that this place was a part of me, that I belonged here.

My stepfather worked at his writing in his study, wreathed in a fog of tobacco smoke, with a bust of Napoleon on his leather-topped desk, while my mother tried her very best to tame the house and the garden and us, mostly on her own. We children were never as much help as we should have been, I'm ashamed to say. There were great inglenook fireplaces that devoured logs. So there were always logs for us to fetch in. Then there were the Bramley apples to pick and lay out in the old Nissen huts in the orchard. And if there was nothing that had to be harvested, or dug over or weeded, then there was the jungle of nettles and brambles that had to be beaten back before it overwhelmed us completely. Above all we had better not disturb our stepfather. When he emerged, his work done for the day, we would play cricket on the front lawn, an apple box for a wicket—it was six points if you hit it over the wall into the village street. If it rained, we moved into the big vaulted barn, where owls and bats and rats and spiders lived, and played fast and furious Ping-Pong until supper.

I slept up in the attic with my elder brother. We had a candle factory up there, melting down the ends of used-up candles on top of a paraffin stove and pouring the wax into jelly molds. At night we could climb out of our dormer windows and sit and listen to the owls screeching over the marshes and to the sound of the surging sea beyond. There always seemed to be butterflies in and out of the house—red admirals, peacocks. I collected dead ones in a cookie tin, laid them out on cotton batting. I kept a wren's nest by my bed, so soft with moss, so beautifully crafted.

My days and nights were filled with the familiarity of the place and its people and of my family. This isn't to say I loved it all. The house was numbingly cold at times. My stepfather could be irritable, rigid, and harsh; my mother anxious, tired, and sad; my younger siblings intrusive and quarrelsome; and the villagers sometimes very aggressive. What haunted me most, though, were stories of a house ghost—told for fun, I'm sure, but nonetheless, that ghost terrified me so much that I dreaded going upstairs at night on my own. But all this was home. Haunted or not, this was my place. I belonged.

The day and the moment came always as a shock. So absorbing was this home life of mine that I'd quite forgotten the existence of my other life. Suddenly I'd find my mother dragging out my school trunk from under the stairs. From that moment on, my stomach started to churn. As my trunk filled, I was counting the days, the hours. The process of packing was relentless. Ironing, mending, counting, marking: eight pairs of gray socks, three pairs of blue rugby shorts, two green rugby shirts,

singing for mrs. pettigrew

two red rugby shirts, green tie, best blazer—red, green, and white striped. Evenings were spent watching my mother and my two spinster aunts sewing on name tags. Every one they sewed on seemed to be cementing the inevitability of my impending expulsion from home. The name tags read: *M. A. B. Morpurgo.* Soon, very soon now, I would be Morpurgo again. Once everything was checked and stitched and darned, the checklist finally ticked off and the trunk ready to go, we drove the trunk to the station to be sent on ahead—luggage in advance, they called it. Where that trunk was going I would surely follow. The next time I'd see it would be only a few days away now, and I'd be back at school. I'd be Morpurgo again.

Those last days hurried by so fast. A last cycle ride to Saint Peter's, a last walk along the seawall, the endless good-byes in the village. "Cheer up, Michael—you'll be home soon." A last supper—shepherd's pie, my favorite. But by this time the condemned boy was not eating at all heartily. A last night of fitful sleep, dreading to wake and face the day ahead. I could not look up at my aunts when I said good-bye for fear they would notice the tears and tell me I was "a big boy and should have grown out of all this by now." I braved their whiskery embraces, and suddenly my mother and I were driving out of the gates, the last chimneys of home disappearing from me behind the trees.

We drove to the station at Southminster. Then we were in London and on the way to Victoria Station on the Underground. She held my hand now, as we sat silently side by side. We'd done this so many times before. She knew better than to talk to me. My mouth was dry, and I felt sick to my stomach. My school uniform, fresh on that morning, was itchy everywhere and constricting. My stepfather had tightened my tie too tight before he said his stiff good-bye and pulled my cap down so hard that it made my ears stick out even more than they usually did.

Going up the escalator into the bustling smoky concourse of Victoria Station was as I imagined it might be going up the steps onto the scaffold to face my executioner. I never wanted to reach the top, because I knew only too well what would be waiting for me. And sure enough, there it was: the first green, white, and red cap; the first familiar face. It was Sim, Simpson, my best friend, but I still didn't want to see him. "Hello, Pongo," he said cheerily. And then to his mother as they walked away: "That's Morpurgo. I told you about him, remember, Mum? He's in my form."

"There," my mother said, in a last desperate effort to console me. "That's your friend. That's Sim, isn't it? It's not so bad, is it?"

What she couldn't know was that it was just about as bad as it could be. Sim was like the others, full of the same hearty cheeriness that would, I know, soon reduce me to tears in the railway car.

The caps and the faces multiplied as we neared the platform. There was the master, ticking the names off his list, Mr. Stevens (math, geography, and woodwork), who rarely smiled at all at school but did so now as he greeted me. I knew even then that the smile was not for me, but rather for the benefit of my mother. "Good to see you back, Morpurgo. He's grown, Mrs. Morpurgo. What've you been feeding him?" And they laughed together over my head. The train stood waiting, breathing, hissing, longing— it seemed—to be gone, longing to take me away.

My mother did not wait, as other mothers did, to wave me off. She knew that to do so would simply be prolonging my agony. Maybe it prolonged hers, too. She kissed me all too briefly, and left me with her face powder on my cheek and the lingering smell of her. I watched her walk away until I could not see her anymore through my tears. I hoped she would turn around and wave one last time, but she didn't. I had a sudden surging impulse to go after her and cling to her and beg her to take me home. But I hadn't the courage to do it.

"Still the dreamer, Morpurgo, I see," said Mr. Stevens. "You'd better get on, or the train'll go without you."

Hauling my suitcase after me, I walked along the corridor searching for a window seat that was still empty. Above everything now I needed a window seat so that I could turn away, so they couldn't see my face. Luckily I found something even better, a completely empty car. I had it all to myself for just a few precious moments before they arrived. They came all at once, in a pack, piling in on top of one another, "bagging" seats, throwing suitcases, full of boisterous jollity. Simpson was there, and Gibbins, Murphy, Sanchez, Webster, Swan, Colman. I did my best to smile at them, but had to look away quickly. They weren't fooled. They'd spotted it. "Aren't you pleased to see us, Morpurgo?" "Don't blub, Pongo." "It's only school." "He wants his mummy wummy." Then Simpson said, "Leave him alone." One thing I had learned was never to rise to the bait. They would stop in time, when they tired of it. And so they did.

As the train pulled out of the station, chuffing and clanking, the talk was all of what they'd done during vacation, where they'd been, what new Hornby train set someone had been given on his birthday. By East Croydon, it was all the old jokes: "Why did the submarine blush?" "Because it saw *Queen Mary*'s bottom!" "Why did the chicken cross the road?" "For some *fowl* reason!" And the carriage rocked with raucous laughter. I looked hard out of my rain-streaked window at the gray green of the Sussex countryside, and cried, silently so that no one would know. But soon enough they did know. "God, Morpurgo, you go on like that and you'll flood the car." All pretense now abandoned, I ran to the toilet, where I could grieve privately and loudly.

At East Grinstead Station, there was the green Southdown coach waiting to take us to school, barely half an hour away. It went by in a minute. Suddenly we were turning in through the great iron gateway and down the gravel drive toward the school. And there it was, looming out of the trees, the dark and forbidding Victorian mansion that would be my prison for fourteen long weeks. With the light on over the front porch, it looked as if the school were some great dark monster with a gaping orange mouth that would swallow me up forever. The headmaster and his wife were there to greet us, both smiling like crocodiles.

Up in my dormitory I found my bed, my name written on it on a sticker—*Morpurgo*. I was back. I sat down, feeling the bed's sagging squeakiness for the first time. That was the moment the idea first came into my head that I should run away. I began unpacking my suitcase, contemplating all the while the dreadful prospect of fourteen weeks away from home. It seemed like I had a life sentence stretching ahead of me with no prospect of remission. Downstairs, outside the dining hall, as we lined up for supper and for the prefects' hand inspection, I felt suddenly overcome by the claustrophobic smell of the place—floor polish and boiled cabbage. Even then I was still only thinking of running away. I had no real intention of doing it, not yet.

It was the rice pudding that made me do it. Major Philips (Latin and rugby) sitting at the end of my table told me I had to finish the slimy rice pudding skin I'd hidden under my spoon. To swallow while I was crying was almost impossible, but somehow I managed it, only to retch it up almost at once. Major Philips told me not to be "childish." I swallowed again and this time kept it down. This was the moment I made up my mind that I'd had enough, that I was going to run away, that nothing and no one would stop me.

"Please, sir," I asked. "Can I go to the toilet, successful?" (Successful, in this context, was school code for number twos. If you declared it before you went, you were allowed longer in the toilet and so were not expected back as soon.) But I didn't go to the toilet, successful or otherwise. Once out of the dining hall, I ran for it. Down the brown-painted corridor between the framed team photos on both walls, past the banter and clatter and clanging of the kitchens, and out of the back door into the courtyard. It was raining hard under a darkening sky as I sprinted down the gravel drive and out through the great iron gates. I had done it! I was free!

I was thinking out my escape plan as I was running and trying to control my sobbing at the same time. I would run the two or three miles to Forest Row, hitch a lift or catch a bus to East Grinstead, and then catch the train home. I still had my term's pocket money with me, a ten-shilling note. I could be home in a few hours. I'd just walk in and tell everyone I was never ever going back to that school, that I would never be Morpurgo ever again.

I had gone a mile or so, still running, still sobbing, when a car came by. I had been so busy planning in my head that I hadn't

I had done it! I was free!

heard the car until it was almost alongside me. My first instinct was to dash off into the fields, for I was sure some master must have seen me escaping and had come after me. I knew full well what would happen if I were caught. It would mean a visit to the headmaster's study and a caning, six strokes at least, but worse still, it would mean capture: back to prison, to rice pudding skin and cabbage, and squeaky beds and math and cross-country runs. One glance at the car, though, told me this was not a master in hot pursuit after all, but a silver-haired old lady in a little black car. She slowed down in front of me and stopped. So I did, too. She wound down her window.

"Are you all right, dear?"

"No." I sobbed.

"You're soaking wet! You'll catch your death!" And then: "You're from that school up the road, aren't you? You're running away, aren't you?"

"Yes."

"Where to?"

"Home."

"Where's home, dear?"

"Essex. By the sea."

"But that's a hundred miles away. Why don't you get in the car, dear? I'll take you home with me. Would you like a sticky bun and some nice hot tea?" And she opened the door for me. There was something about her I trusted at once, the gentleness of her smile, perhaps, the softness of her voice. That was why I got in, I think. Or maybe it was for the sticky bun. The truth was that I'd suddenly lost heart, suddenly had enough of my great escape. I was cold and wet, and home seemed as far away as the moon, and just as inaccessible.

The car was warm inside, and smelled of leather and dog.

"It's not far, dear. Half a mile, that's all. Just in the village. Oh, and this is Jack. He's perfectly friendly." And by way of introducing himself, the dog in the back began to snuffle the back of my neck. He was a spaniel with long dangly ears and sad bloodshot eyes. And he dribbled a lot.

All the way back to the village, the old lady talked on, about Jack mostly. Jack was ten, in dog years, she told me. If you multiplied by seven, exactly the same age as she was. "One of the windshield wipers," she said, "only works when it feels like it, and it never feels like it when it's raining."

I sat and listened and had my neck washed from ear to ear by

Jack. It tickled and made me smile. "That's better, dear," she said. "Happier now?"

She gave me more than she'd promised—a whole plate of sticky buns and several cups of tea. She put my soaking wet shoes in the oven to dry and hung my blazer on the clothes-horse by the stove, and she talked all the time, telling me all about herself, how she lived alone these days, how she missed company. Her husband had been killed on the Somme in 1916, in the First World War. "Jimmy was a Grenadier Guardsman," she said proudly. "Six foot three in his socks." She showed me his photo on the mantelpiece. He had a mustache and lots of medals. "Loved his fishing," she went on. "Loved the sea. We went to the sea whenever we could. Brighton. Lovely place." On and on she rambled, talking me through her life with Jimmy, and how she'd stayed on in the village after he'd been killed because it was the place they'd known together, how she'd taught in the village school for years before she retired. When the sticky buns were all finished and my shoes were out of the oven and dry at last, she sat back, clapped her hands on her knees, and said:

"Now, dear, what *are* we going to do with you?"

"I don't know," I replied.

"Shall I telephone your father and mother?"

"No!" I cried. The thought appalled me. They'd be so disappointed in me, so ashamed to know that I'd tried to run away.

"Well then, shall I ring the headmaster?"

"No! Please don't." That would be worse still. I'd be up the red-carpeted stairs into his study. I'd been there before all too often. I'd bent over the leather armchair and watched him pull out the cane from behind his desk. I'd waited for the swish and whack; felt the hot searing pain, the stinging eyes; and counted to six. I'd stood up, trembling, to shake his hand and murmured, "Thank you, sir," through my weeping mouth. No, not that. Please, not that.

"Maybe," said the old lady. "Maybe there's a way around this. You can't have been gone long, an hour or so at most. What if I take you back and drop you off at the top of the school drive? It's nearly dark now. No one would see you, not if you were careful. And with a bit of luck no one would have missed you just yet. You could sneak in and no one would ever know you've run away at all. What d'you think?"

I could have hugged her.

Jack came in the car with us in the back seat, licking my neck and my ears all the way. The old lady was unusually silent for a while. Then she said: "There's something Jimmy once told me not long before he was killed, when he was home on leave for the last time. He never talked much about the war and the trenches, but he did tell me once how scared he was all the time, how scared they all were. So I asked him what made him go on, why he didn't just run away. And he said: 'Because of my pals. We're in this together. We look after each other.' You've got pals, haven't you, dear?"

"Yes," I replied, "but they *like* coming back to school. They *love* it."

"I wonder if they really do," she said. "Maybe they just pretend better than you."

I was still thinking about that when the car came to a stop.

"I won't go any nearer than this, dear. It wouldn't do for anyone to see you getting out, would it now? Off you go then. And chin up, like my Jimmy."

Jack gave me a good-bye lick on my nose as I turned to him.

"Thanks for the sticky buns," I said.

She smiled at me, and I got out. I watched her drive away into the gloom and vanish. To this day I have no idea who she was. I never saw her again.

I ran down through the rhododendrons and out into the deserted courtyard at the back of the school. The lights were on all over the building, and the place was alive with the sound of children. I knew I needed time to compose myself before I met anyone, so I opened the chapel door and slipped into its enveloping darkness. There I sat and prayed, prayed that I hadn't been found out, that I wouldn't have to face the red-carpeted stairs and the headmaster's study and the leather chair. I hadn't been in there for more than a few minutes when the door opened and the lights went on.

"Ah, there you are, Morpurgo." It was Mr. Morgan (French and music, and the choirmaster, too). "We've been looking all over for you." As he came up the aisle toward me, I knew my prayers had been answered. Mr. Morgan was much liked by all of us, because he was invariably kind and always thought the best of us — rare in that school.

"Bit homesick, are you, Morpurgo?"

"Yes, sir."

"It'll pass. You'll see." He put his hand on my shoulder.

"You'd better get yourself upstairs with the others. If you don't get your trunk unpacked by lights out, Matron will eat you alive, and we don't want that, do we?"

"No, sir."

And so I left Mr. Morgan and the chapel and went upstairs to my dormitory.

"Where've you been? I thought you'd scarpered, run away," said Simpson, unpacking his trunk on the bed next to mine.

"I just felt a bit sick," I said. Then I opened my trunk. On the top of my clothes was a note and three bars of Cadbury's chocolate. The note read: *Have a good term. Love, Mum.*

Simpson spotted the chocolate and pounced. Suddenly everyone in the dormitory was around me and at my chocolate, like gannets. I managed to keep a little back for myself, which I hid under my pillow, and ate late that night as I listened to the bell in the clock tower chiming midnight. As it finished, I heard Simpson crying to himself, as silently as he could.

"You all right, Sim?" I whispered.

"Fine," he sniffed. And then: "Pongo, did you scarper?"

"Yes," I said.

"Next time you go, take me with you. Promise?"

"Promise," I replied.

But I never did scarper again. Perhaps I never again plucked up the courage; perhaps I listened to the old lady's advice. I've certainly never forgotten it. It was my one and only great escape. ✢

where the heart is

Only a hundred years ago it was more than likely that you would die in the very house you were born in, in the same bed even, that your home was your place for a lifetime. You lived cheek by jowl with your family; Grandma slept next door, Uncle Jack just up the street. You went to school down the road, often with your cousins, fished in the same streams, filched apples from the same orchards. You went to the same church or chapel, even worked where they worked, down the same mine, in the same factory, on the same farm. Your roots grew deep. And when the time came, like as not you'd be buried alongside them, too. All this was home. All this was your shell. Home was family. You were born into it. It might be a squalid, hateful, and hopeless place, a slough of despond, a lifelong curse, or a place of love and warmth and companionship, the greatest of blessings—home can have elements of both. Either way, curse or blessing, it was home, the place you were rooted.

Now many of us have the freedom to choose to stay where we were brought up or to leave, to work and live somewhere else if we want to. But does this newfound freedom diminish our sense of home and belonging and make us less secure? Do we in fact really need to belong anywhere? Can we feel that we belong everywhere?

Home for many of us, I imagine, will always be our childhood home. As you have just read in "My One and Only
Great Escape," I lived for most of my formative years on the
Essex coast in a village called Bradwell. I have chosen this
extract from that story to illustrate the intensity of the belonging I felt then and still feel today.

Cycling out of the gate, as I often did, I turned left
onto the village street toward Bradwell Quay and the
sea, right toward the church, and the American air
base, and then out over the marshes toward the ancient
Saxon chapel of Saint Peter's near the seawall itself.
Climb the seawall and there was the great brown,
soupy North Sea and always a wild, wet wind blowing. I felt that this place was a part of me, that I
belonged here. . . .

I slept up in the attic with my elder brother. We
had a candle factory up there, melting down the ends
of used-up candles on top of a paraffin stove and
pouring the wax into jelly molds. At night we could
climb out of our dormer windows and sit and listen to
the owls screeching over the marshes and to the sound
of the surging sea beyond. . . .

My days and nights were filled with the familiarity
of the place and its people and of my family. This isn't
to say I loved it all. The house was numbingly cold at
times. My stepfather could be irritable, rigid, and
harsh; my mother anxious, tired, and sad; my younger
siblings intrusive and quarrelsome; and the villagers
sometimes very aggressive. What haunted me most,
though, were stories of a house ghost—told for fun,

I'm sure, but nonetheless, that ghost terrified me so
much that I dreaded going upstairs at night on my
own. But all this was home. Haunted or not, this was
my place. I belonged.

All the homes I have made on my wanderings have been in
some way, I suppose, attempts to re-create those distant years of
childhood, to find once more that elusive sense of belonging. I
have been back to the house at Bradwell. Someone else sleeps
in my room now. But it will always be my room, my place. A
part of me still belongs there, the heart of me perhaps.

I live now in a small Devon village that has been my home
for over thirty years—for my children their childhood home,
for me another kind of home altogether, a place I live and
work in, a place I love but still I cannot say I belong to. But
strangely, living here over these last thirty-plus years I have
learned more about belonging than I have anywhere else.

My village, like so many English villages, has undergone
huge change. Until recently, those who were born here outnum-
bered the newcomers, outsiders like me. Not anymore. Most of
the farms, though, are still owned and worked by the children
who grew up on them a generation ago. These people have an
understanding of the place and the beasts and the people, an
understanding born of long association. They feel part of the
land they inhabit. It is an understanding learned not from books
and poetry but simply by being here, by growing up here.
Thomas Hardy wrote of this better than anyone, I think:

They are old association—an almost exhaustive bio-
graphical or historical acquaintance with every object,
animate and inanimate, within the observer's horizon.

He must know all about those invisible ones of the days gone by, whose feet have traversed the fields which look so gray from his windows; recall whose creaking plough has turned those sods from time to time; whose hands planted the trees that form a crest to the opposite hill; whose horses and hounds have torn through that underwood; what birds affect that particular brake; what domestic dramas of love, jealousy, revenge, or disappointment have been enacted in the cottages, the mansion, the street, or on the green. The spot may have beauty, grandeur, salubrity, convenience; but if it lack memories it will ultimately pall upon him who settles there without opportunity of intercourse with his kind.

From *The Woodlanders*

There are some, of course, who see and feel this belonging as a right to possess the land. But to feel that a place is your home, it is not at all necessary to own it. Most of those who have lived in my village all through the ages since Saxon times have had a strong sense, I feel sure, that this was their place to be, to use, certainly, but to look after and to cherish, too. Hedgerows, ditches, trees, and meadows are witness to this. They made the landscape we see today. Most never owned a blade of grass, much less the roof over their heads. Perhaps they understood more instinctively than we do now in this great age of owner⁄ship that possession is only temporary anyway.

To Sean Rafferty, Scottish poet, playwright, and pub⁄lican, who made his home in our village in the 1940s, belonging was utterly important. I don't think he particularly wanted to come and live here in the first place—he was more

at home in Fitzroy Square in London or among fellow poets
like Sorley MacLean in Scotland—but nonetheless he estab-
lished a profound connection with the village and its people.
The pub where he worked stands next to the church. He was
up early every morning, at cockcrow.

I SPEAK OF A VALLEY
by Sean Rafferty

I speak of a valley.

I call at morning

the roll of its farms

till cocks reply.

From the cobbled yards

they cry and eastwards

the first leaf stirs

in a hush of doves.

I speak of a river.

I herd the fleece bright

flock of its springs

till driven streams

are loud in the fold

I lead its waters

to praise among pastures

their hartstongue home.

I speak of a childhood.

I lay a nightlong

fable of sleep

till morning sang

in the green of the light

between leaf and language

a birth a ballad

a bird alone.

Ballad and childhood

and psalm and river

in the cup of my hands

I priest its praise;

I speak of a valley

and shall for ever

out of my numbered days.

Ted Hughes came to his pub. They talked poetry over
the bar. Hughes fished the river, too, the Torridge, the same
river Tarka the otter fished. Ted Hughes farmed nearby at
Moortown. He knew the landscape intimately, lived in harmony with it, became a part of it as John Clare had in
Suffolk, as William Wordsworth had in the Lakes. Here's
part of Ted Hughes's poem "Last Load," his song of harvest
home.

From LAST LOAD
by Ted Hughes

And now as you dash through the green light

You see between dark trees

On all the little emerald hills

The desperate loading, under the blue cloud.

Your sweat tracks through your dust, your shirt flaps chill,

And bales multiply out of each other

All down the shorn field ahead.

The faster you fling them up, the more there are of them—

Till suddenly the field's grey empty. It's finished.

And a tobacco reek breaks in your nostrils

As the rain begins

Softly and vertically silver, the whole sky softly

Falling into the stubble all round you

The trees shake out their masses, joyful,

Drinking the downpour.

The hills pearled, the whole distance drinking

And the earth-smell warm and thick as smoke

And you go, and over the whole land

Like singing heard across evening water

The tall loads are swaying toward their barns

Down the deep lanes.

June 20, 1975

Are all these writings in some way mere striving to belong? Perhaps, though I think they are more than that. I see in them almost a sense of kinship, a kinship arrived at through observation, insight, and empathy, by an intensity of association. It is this sense of association that binds us together, as families and as communities. And it is in this place, and has been among these writers, that I write, on my bed propped up by a mountain of pillows, just as Robert Louis Stevenson did on Samoa, an island in the Pacific where he felt he belonged, where he  still belongs, for he died there and is buried there. Another kind of belonging. ⎯

my father is a polar bear

Tracking down a polar bear shouldn't be that difficult. You just follow the paw prints. My father is a polar bear. Now if you had a father who was a polar bear, you'd be curious, wouldn't you? You'd go looking for him. That's what I did; I went looking for him, and I'm telling you he wasn't at all easy to find.

In a way I was lucky, because I always had two fathers. I had a father who *was* there—I called him Douglas—and one who wasn't there, the one I'd never even met—the polar bear one. Yet in a way he was there. All the time I was growing up, he was there inside my head. But he wasn't only in my head; he was at the bottom of our Start-rite shoe box, our secret treasure box, with the rubber bands around it, which I kept hidden at the bottom of the closet in our bedroom. So how, you might ask, does a polar bear fit into a shoe box? I'll tell you.

My big brother, Terry, first showed me the magazine under the bedclothes, by flashlight, in 1948, when I was five years old. The magazine was called *Theatre World*. I couldn't read it at the time, but he could. (He was two years older than me, and already mad about acting and the theater and all that—he still is.) He had saved up all his pocket money to buy it. I thought he was crazy. "A shilling! You can get about a hundred lemon sherbets for that down at the shop," I told him.

Terry just ignored me and turned to page twenty-seven. He read it out: "'*The Snow Queen*, a dramat—something or other—of Hans Andersen's famous story, by the Young Vic Company.'" And there was a large black-and-white photograph right across the page—a photograph of two fierce-looking polar bears baring their teeth and about to eat two children, a boy and a girl, who looked very frightened.

"Look at the polar bears," said Terry. "You see that one on the left, the fatter one? That's our dad, our real dad. It says his name and everything—Peter Van Diemen. But you're not to tell. Not Douglas, not even Mum, promise?"

"My dad's a polar bear?" I said. I was a little confused.

"Promise you won't tell," he went on, "or I'll give you a Chinese burn."

Of course I wasn't going to tell, Chinese burn or no Chinese burn. I was hardly going to go to school the next day and tell everyone that I had a polar bear for a father, was I? And I certainly couldn't tell my mother, because I knew she never liked it if I ever asked about my real father. She always insisted that Douglas was the only father I had. I knew he wasn't, not really. So did she; so did Terry; so did Douglas. But for some reason that was always a complete mystery to me, everyone in the house pretended that he was.

Some background might be useful here. I was born, I later found out, when my father was a soldier in Baghdad during the Second World War. (You didn't know there were polar bears in Baghdad, did you?) Sometime after that, my mother met and fell in love with a dashing young officer in the Royal Marines called Douglas Macleish. All this time, evacuated to the Lake District away from the bombs, blissfully unaware of the war and Douglas, I was learning to walk and talk and do my business in the right place at the right time. So my father came home from the war to discover that his place in my mother's heart had been taken. He did all he could to win her back. He took her away on a week's cycling holiday in Suffolk to see if he could rekindle the light of their love. But it was hopeless. By the end of the week, they had come to an amicable arrangement. My father would simply disappear, because he didn't want to "get in the way." They would get divorced quickly and quietly, so that Terry and I could be brought up as a new family with Douglas as our father. Douglas would adopt us and give us Macleish as our surname. All my father insisted upon was that Terry and I should keep Van Diemen as our middle name. That's what happened. They divorced. My father disappeared, and at the age of three I became Andrew Van Diemen Macleish. It was a mouthful then and it's a mouthful now.

So Terry and I had no actual memories of our father whatsoever. I do have some vague recollections of standing on a railway bridge somewhere near Earls Court in London, where we lived, with Douglas's sister—Aunty Betty, as I came to know her—telling us that we had a brand-new father who'd be looking after us from now on. I was really not that concerned, not at the time. I was much more interested in the train that was chuffing along under the bridge, wreathing us in a fog of smoke.

My first father, my real father, my missing father, became a taboo person, a big hush-hush taboo person that no one ever mentioned, except for Terry and me. For us he soon became a sort of secret phantom father. We used to whisper about him under the blankets at night. Terry would sometimes go snooping in my mother's desk, and he'd find things out about him. "He's an actor," Terry told me one night. "Our dad's an actor, just like Mum is, just like I'm going to be."

It was only a couple of weeks later that he brought the theater magazine home. After that we'd take it out again and look at our polar bear father. It took some time, I remember, before the truth of it dawned on me—I don't think Terry can have explained it very well. If he had, I'd have understood it much sooner—I'm sure I would. The truth, of course—as I think you might have guessed by now—was that my father was both an actor *and* a polar bear at one and the same time.

Douglas went out to work a lot, and when he was home, he was a bit silent, so we didn't really get to know him. But we did get to know Aunty Betty. Aunty Betty simply adored us, and she loved giving us treats. She wanted to take us on a special Christmas treat, she said. Would we like to go to the zoo? Would we like to go to the pantomime? There was *Dick Whittington* or *Puss in Boots*. We could choose whatever we liked.

Quick as a flash, Terry said, "*The Snow Queen*. We want to go to *The Snow Queen*."

So there we were a few days later, Christmas Eve 1948, sitting in the stalls at a matinée performance of *The Snow Queen* at the Young Vic theater, waiting, waiting for the moment when the polar bears would come on. We didn't have to wait for long. Terry nudged me and pointed, but I knew already which polar bear my father had to be. He was the best one, the snarliest one, the growliest one, the scariest one. Whenever he came on, he really looked as if he were going to eat someone, anyone. He looked mean and hungry and savage, just the way a polar bear should look.

I have no idea whatsoever what happened in *The Snow Queen*. I just could not take my eyes off my polar-bear father's curling claws, his slavering tongue, his killer eyes. My father was without doubt the finest polar bear–actor the world had ever seen. When the great red curtains closed at the end and opened again for the actors to take their bows, I clapped so hard that my hands hurt. Three more curtain calls and the curtains stayed closed. The fire curtain came down and my father was cut off from me, gone, gone forever. I'd never see him again.

Terry had other ideas. Everyone was getting up, but Terry stayed sitting. He was staring at the fire curtain as if in some kind of trance. "I want to meet the polar bears," he said quietly.

Aunty Betty laughed. "They're not bears, dear; they're actors,

He looked mean and hungry and savage, just the way a polar bear should look.

just actors, people acting. And you can't meet them; it's not allowed."

"I want to meet the polar bears," Terry repeated.

So did I, of course, so I joined in. "Please, Aunty Betty," I pleaded. "Please."

"Don't be silly. You two, you do get some silly notions sometimes. Have an ice cream instead. Get your coats on now."

So we each got an ice cream. But that wasn't the end of it.

We were in the foyer, caught in the crush of the crowd, when Aunty Betty suddenly noticed that Terry was missing. She went loopy. Aunty Betty always wore a fox stole, heads still attached, around her shoulders. Those poor old foxes looked every bit as pop-eyed and frantic as she did, as she plunged through the crowd, dragging me along behind her and calling for Terry.

Gradually the theater emptied. Still no Terry. There was quite a to-do, I can tell you. Policemen were called in off the street. All the program sellers joined in the search; everyone did. Of course, I'd worked it out. I knew exactly where Terry had gone, and what he was up to. By now Aunty Betty was sitting down in the foyer and sobbing her heart out. Then, cool as a cucumber, Terry appeared from nowhere, just wandered into the foyer. Aunty Betty crushed him to her, in a great hug. Then she went loopy all over again, telling him what a naughty, naughty boy he was, going off like that. "Where were you? Where have you been?" she cried.

"Yes, young man," said one of the policemen. "That's something we'd all like to know as well."

I remember to this day exactly what Terry said, the very words: "To the loo. I just went to the loo." For a moment he even had me believing him. What an actor! Brilliant.

We were on the bus home, right at the front on the top deck, where you can guide the bus around corners all by yourself—all you have to do is steer hard on the white bar in front of you. Aunty Betty was sitting a couple of rows behind us. Terry made quite sure she wasn't looking. Then, very surreptitiously, he took something out from under his coat and showed me. The program. Signed right across it were these words, which Terry read out to me:

To Terry and Andrew,
With love from your polar-bear father, Peter. Keep happy.

Night after night I asked Terry about him, and night after night under the blankets he'd tell me the story again, about how he'd gone into the dressing room and found our father sitting there in his polar-bear costume with his head off (if you know what I mean), all hot and sweaty. Terry said he had a very round, very smiley face, and that he laughed just like a bear would laugh, a sort of deep bellow of a laugh—when he'd gotten over the surprise, that is. Terry described him as looking like a "giant pixie in a bearskin."

Forever afterward, I always held it against Terry that he never took me with him that day down to the dressing room to meet my polar-bear father. I was so envious. Terry had a memory of him now, a real memory. And I didn't. All I had were a few words and a signature on a theater program from someone I'd never even met, someone who to me was part polar bear, part actor, part pixie—not at all easy to picture in my head as I grew up.

Picture another Christmas Eve fourteen years later. Upstairs, still at the bottom of my closet, my polar-bear father in the magazine in the Start-rite shoe box, and with him all our accumulated childhood treasures: the signed program, a battered horse chestnut, six silver ball bearings, four greenish silver threepenny bits (Christmas pudding treasure trove), a Red Devil throat pastille tin with three of my baby teeth cushioned in yellow cotton batting, and my collection of twenty-seven cowrie shells gleaned over many summers from the beach on Samson in the Scilly Isles.

singing for mrs. pettigrew

Downstairs, the whole family was gathered in the sitting room: my mother, Douglas, Terry and my two sisters (half sisters really, but of course no one ever called them that), Aunty Betty, now married, with twin daughters, my cousins, who were truly awful—I promise you. We were decorating the tree, or rather the twins were fighting over every single dingly-dangly glitter ball, every strand of tinsel. I was trying to fix up the Christmas-tree lights which, of course, wouldn't work—again—while Aunty Betty was doing her best to avert a war by bribing the dreadful cousins away from the tree with a Mars Bar each. It took a while, but in the end she got both of them up onto her lap, and soon they were stuffing themselves contentedly with Mars Bars. Blessed peace.

This was the very first Christmas we had had the television. Given half a chance, we'd have had it on all the time. But, wisely enough, I suppose, Douglas had rationed us to just one program a day over Christmas. He didn't want the Christmas celebrations interfered with by "that thing in the corner," as he called it. By common consent, we had chosen the Christmas Eve film at five o'clock.

Five o'clock was a very long time coming that day, and when at last Douglas got up and turned on the television, it seemed to take forever to warm up. Then, there it was on the screen: *Great*

Expectations by Charles Dickens. The half-mended lights were at once discarded, the decorating abandoned, as we all settled down to watch in rapt anticipation. Maybe you know the moment: Young Pip is making his way through the graveyard at dusk, mist swirling around him, an owl screeching, gravestones rearing out of the gloom, branches like ghoulish fingers whipping at him as he passes, reaching out to snatch him. He moves through the graveyard timorously, tentatively, like a frightened fawn. Every snap of a twig, every barking fox, every *aarking* heron, sends shivers into our very souls.

Suddenly, a face! A hideous face, a monstrous face, looms up from behind a gravestone. Magwitch, the escaped convict—ancient, craggy and crooked, with long white hair and a straggly beard. A wild man with wild eyes, the eyes of a wolf.

The cousins screamed in unison, long and loud, which broke the tension for all of us and made us laugh. All except my mother.

"Oh, my God," she breathed, grasping my arm. "That's your father! It is. It's him. It's Peter."

All the years of pretense, the whole long conspiracy of silence, were undone in that one moment. The drama on the television paled into sudden insignificance. The hush in the room was palpable.

Douglas coughed. "I think I'll fetch some more logs," he said. And my two half sisters went out with him, in solidarity I think. So did Aunty Betty and the twins, and that left my mother, Terry, and me alone together.

I could not take my eyes off the screen. After a while I said to Terry, "He doesn't look much like a pixie to me."

"Doesn't look much like a polar bear, either," Terry replied. At Magwitch's every appearance I tried to see through his makeup (I just hoped it *was* makeup!) to discover how my father really looked. It was impossible. My polar-bear father, my pixie father, had become my convict father.

Until the credits came up at the end, my mother never said a word. Then all she said was, "Well, the potatoes won't peel themselves, and I've got the Brussels sprouts to do as well." Christmas was a very subdued affair that year, I can tell you.

They say you can't put a genie back in the bottle. Not true. No one in the family ever spoke of the incident afterward— except Terry and me, of course. Everyone behaved as if it had never happened. Enough was enough. Terry and I decided it was time to broach the whole forbidden subject with our mother in private. We waited until the furor of Christmas was over and caught her alone in the kitchen one evening. We asked her point-blank to tell us about him, our "first" father, our "missing" father.

"I don't want to talk about him," she said. She wouldn't even look at us. "All I know is that he lives somewhere in Canada now. It was another life. I was another person then. It's not important." We tried to press her, but that was all she would tell us.

Soon after this I became very busy with my own life, and for some years I thought very little about my convict father, my polar-bear father. By the time I was thirty, I was married with two sons, and was a teacher trying to become a writer, something I had never dreamed I could be.

Terry had become an actor, something he had always been quite sure he would be. He rang me very late one night in a high state of excitement. "You'll never guess," he said. "He's here! Peter! Our dad. He's here, in England. He's playing in *Henry IV, Part II,* in Chichester. I've just read a rave review. He's Falstaff. Why don't we go down there and give him the surprise of his life?"

So we did. The next weekend, we went down to Chichester together. I took my family with me. I wanted them to be there for this. He was a wonderful Falstaff, big and boomy, rambunctious and raunchy, yet full of pathos. My two boys (ten and eight) kept whispering at me every time he came on, "Is that him? Is that him?" Afterward we went round to see him in his dressing room. Terry said I should go in first, and on my own. "I had my turn a long time ago, if you remember," he said. "Best if he sees just one of us to start with, I reckon."

My heart was in my mouth. I had to take a very deep breath before I knocked on that door. "Enter." He sounded still jovial, still Falstaffian. I went in.

He was sitting at his dressing table in his vest and suspenders, boots and britches, humming to himself as he rubbed off his makeup. We looked at each other in the mirror. He stopped humming, and swiveled around to face me. For some moments I just stood there looking at him. Then I said, "Were you a polar bear once, a long time ago in London?"

"Yes."

"And were you once the convict in *Great Expectations* on the television?"

"Yes."

"Then I think I'm your son," I told him.

There was a lot of hugging in his dressing room that night, not enough to make up for all those missing years, maybe. But it was a start.

My mother's dead now, bless her heart, but I still have two fathers. I get on well enough with Douglas; I always have, in a detached sort of way. He's done his best by me; I know that, but in all the years I've known him, he's never once mentioned my other father. It doesn't matter now. It's history best left crusted over, I think.

We see my polar-bear father—I still think of him as that—every year or so, whenever he's over from Canada. He's well past eighty now, still acting for six months of every year—a real trouper. My children and my grandchildren always call him Grandpa Bear because of his great bushy beard (the same one he grew for Falstaff!), and because they all know the story of their grandfather, I suppose.

Recently I wrote a story about a polar bear. I can't imagine why. He's upstairs now reading it to my smallest granddaughter. I can hear him a-snarling and a-growling just as proper polar bears do. Takes him back, I should think. Takes me back—that's for sure. +

go west, young man

As I have already said, moving to the West Country all those years ago proved to be a significant moment in my writing life, a moment when I was just beginning to find my own voice as a storyteller. Looking back now, I can see that until then my writing efforts had been very much plot driven, with me doing the driving. I was making things happen, arranging matters all too conveniently, controlling events too tightly, like some god of the ancient Greeks, unwilling to allow the story to unfold organically, to give free rein to the characters I had created and, more importantly, still unwilling to grant power to the landscape and history and culture that had shaped them in the first place. I had used background in the same manner as a jobbing portrait painter, without grasping that my characters had been shaped by this background, that it really had made them who they were.

I suppose I hadn't realized this because I had not lived it myself, and that was because I had never stayed long enough in one place to comprehend just how powerful and profound this sense of place, of belonging, might be in our lives. Now I found myself immersed in the same landscape, in the same remote rural culture that had inspired Henry Williamson, where Tarka the otter had cavorted and gamboled along the banks of the River Torridge, which I could now hear from my bedroom window, which I saw in flood and drought, where I went walking and fishing, watched herons lift off and kingfishers flash by. I worked in the fields with the farmers; did my share of hay making and mucking about and lambing; rang the bells in church; listened to songs and stories in the pub in Iddesleigh; became part of the bustle and banter of the market day in Hatherleigh; spent evenings by the fire, the wind roaring about the chimney, rain lashing the windows; read the poems of my writing neighbors and friends, Ted Hughes and Sean Rafferty, who like me had breathed in this place and allowed it to become a part of them.

Three books grew out of this burgeoning sense of belonging. The first was simply a diary of the farm on which I worked. With Ted Hughes writing a poem for each month, I followed the fickle fortunes of a small Devon family farm, recorded the constant struggle through the seasons, the triumph of a harvest done, the disappointment of a calf born dead. I called it *All Around the Year.* It was a book that made me look and listen, made me ask why, made me begin to understand, made me long to belong. From all this there came *War Horse,* a novel of the First World War, set on a farm in my village of Iddesleigh and on the Western Front. I discovered there were three octogenarians living in the village who had been in the First World War, two with cavalry regiments. There had been, they told me, a sale of horses outside the pub in 1914, when the army came looking to buy sturdy farm horses. People still remembered that the army had paid top prices for the best horses. Millions of horses went off to that war and very few returned. And many of those that survived the horrors of mud and shells and disease were sold off to French butchers in 1918—a more profitable way of disposal,

I suppose. And when, some twenty years later, I came to write *Private Peaceful,* the story of two brothers who are bullied by the squire in the village to "volunteer" in the First World War, it seemed the most natural thing in the world for the brothers to grow up in my cottage, down my deep lane, fish in my river, go to my church and my pub. By now I could feel, if not a sense of belonging, at least a kinship for Devon in my bones, in my being.

Wherever I went in the West Country now, I felt a fascination for the communities I came across and the stories that had made them, stories that seemed to emerge from the rocks and caves, from the moors and tors. We vacationed in a cottage in Zennor, the same cottage below the Eagle's Nest where Katherine Mansfield had written in her leaky bedroom (the roof still leaked), and where D. H. Lawrence had written, too. We traipsed across the high moors; came across stories of the ghosts of trapped tin miners, knockers they were called, still lurking down in the lodes and caverns that honeycombed the cliffs; met a white horse in a dense fog who passed us by in the bracken, looking at us as if we were intruders into the world in which he lived. I sat down the next day after this strange meeting and wrote a short story called "The White Horse of Zennor."

Scilly beckoned then—as far west as you can go in England—that scattering of islands stranded out in the Atlantic beyond Land's End. "The Fortunate Isles" they call them, and so they are—a place of wild beauty, of white beaches and green sea, oystercatchers and gannets, perfect for family holidays, which is why we went there. I did not go looking for stories. I never do; but I do go to places where they might find me—on Scilly the story of poor, benighted

Samson Island, where hunger and despair had driven the people away, of stranded whales and turtles, of wrecks and pirates and of ancient legends, too. Fishermen on Scilly talk of a warning bell that tolls under the sea in the fog off the Eastern Isles. One of these now-uninhabited islands lies there in the sea like some sleeping warrior king, waiting through the centuries to awake when his time comes—to me he's always been King Arthur. Tennyson himself came here looking for inspiration for his Arthurian poems. As we know, he found it. So did I. I called mine *Arthur, High King of Britain.* There was *Why the Whales Came,* too, and *The Wreck of the Zanzibar* and *The Sleeping Sword.* All of these Scillonian stories of mine grew out of the lives of the people who have lived and belonged on Scilly and who still live there, still belong there, as I do—but only in part.

And that in a sense is the strangest and saddest aspect of all of this. By writing about a place I know and love as I do, I can imagine myself to be part of this place—its past, its landscape, its people. As I am writing, I can believe I belong, but once the story is written, that sense of kinship quickly disappears. Each time, I realize, has been an illusion, a necessary illusion, but a mirage all the same, for the truth is that I have perhaps been in love with these places, but I do not belong and have never belonged, not really. I am an observer, an interloper, an outsider looking in, finally just a writer and a storyteller. But that's all right. That's what I do. And what I do, I am, in part.

In one sense only I feel I have achieved some belonging. I know it lying under the stars on a summer's night. I know it watching buzzards floating over the valley where I live in Devon. I know it walking along the riverbank and seeing a

salmon rise. I have written often about this elemental connec- go west, young man
tion and empathy with the natural world in *Why the Whales*
Came, in *Kensuke's Kingdom* and *Little Foxes.*
It is a learned belonging—from Ted
Hughes, from Wordsworth, from chil-
dren who stop to gaze, to breathe in the
world about them, to feel part of it, as in
The Silver Swan.

the silver swan

The silver swan, who living had no note,
When death approached, unlocked her silent throat:
Leaning her breast against the reedy shore
Thus sung her first and last, and sung no more.

Orlando Gibbons

A swan came to my lake one day, a silver swan. I was fishing for trout in the moonlight. She came flying in above me, her wings singing in the air. She circled the lake twice and then landed, sil‑ver, silver in the moonlight.

I stood and watched her as she arranged her wings behind her and sailed out over the lake, making it entirely her own. I stayed as late as I could, quite unable to leave her.

I went down to the lake every day after that, but not to fish for trout, simply to watch my silver swan.

In those early days I took great care not to frighten her away, keeping myself still and hidden in the shadow of the alders. But even so, she knew I was there—I was sure of it.

Within a week I would find her cruising along the lakeside, waiting for me when I arrived in the early mornings. I took to bringing some bread crusts with me. She would look sideways at them at first, rather disdainfully. Then, after a while, she reached out her neck, snatched them out of the water, and made off with them in triumph.

One day I dared to dunk the bread crusts for her, dared to try to feed her by hand. She took all I offered her and came back for more. She was coming close enough now for me to be able to touch her neck. I would talk to her as I stroked her. She really listened; I know she did.

I never saw the cob arrive. He was just there swimming beside her one morning out on the lake. You could see the love between them even then. The princess of the lake had found her prince. When they drank, they dipped their necks together, as one. When they flew, their wings beat together, as one.

She knew I was there, I think, still watching. But she did not come to see me again, nor to have her bread crusts. I tried to be more glad for her than sad for me, but it was hard.

As winter tried, and failed, to turn to spring, they began to make a home on the small island, way out in the middle of the lake. I could watch them now only through my binoculars. I was there every day I could be—no matter what the weather.

Things were happening. They were no longer busy just preening themselves, or feeding, or simply gliding out over the lake, taking their reflections with them. Between them they were building a nest—a clumsy, messy excuse for a nest, it seemed to me—set on a reedy knoll near the shore of their island.

It took them several days to construct. Neither ever seemed quite satisfied with the other's work. A twig was too big, or too small, or perhaps just not in the right place. There were no argu-ments as such, as far as I could see. But my silver swan would rearrange things, tactfully, when her cob wasn't there. And he would do the same when she wasn't there.

Then, one bright cold morning, with the ground beneath my feet hard with a late and unexpected frost, I arrived to see my sil-ver swan enthroned at last on her nest, her cob proudly patroling the lake close by.

I knew there were foxes about. I had heard their cries often enough, echoing through the night. I had seen their footprints in the snow. But I had never seen one out and about until now.

It was dusk. I was on my way back home from the lake, coming up through the woods, when I spotted a family of five kits,
their mother sitting on guard nearby. Unseen and unsmelled, I
crouched down where I was and watched.

I could see at once that they were starving, some of them
already too weak even to pester their mother for food. But I could
see, too, that she had none to give—she was thin and rangy herself. I remember thinking then: That's one family of foxes that's
not likely to make it, not if the spring doesn't come soon, not if
this winter goes on much longer.

But the winter did go on that year, on and on.

I thought little more of the foxes. My mind was on other
things, more important things. My silver swan and her cob
shared the sitting duties and the guarding duties, never leaving
the precious nest long enough for me even to catch sight of the
eggs, let alone count them. But I could count the days, and I did.

As the day approached, I made up my mind that I would
go down to the lake, no matter what, and stay there until it
happened—however long that might take. But the great day
dawned foggy. Out my bedroom window, I could barely see
across the farmyard.

I ran all the way down to the lake. From the lakeside I could see nothing of the island, nothing of the lake, only a few feet of limpid gray water lapping at the muddy shore. I could hear the muffled *aarking* of a heron out in the fog and the distant piping of a moorhen. But I stayed to keep watch, all that day, all the next.

I was there in the morning two days later when the fog began at last to lift and the pale sun to come through. The island was there again. I turned my binoculars at once on the nest. It was deserted. They were gone. I scanned the lake, still mist-covered in places. Not a ripple. Nothing.

Then out of nothing they appeared, my silver swan, her cob, and four cygnets, coming straight toward me. As they came toward the shore, they turned and sailed right past me. I swear she was showing them to me, parading them. She and her cob both swam with such easy power, the cygnets bobbing along in their wake. But I had counted wrong. There was another one, hitching a ride in among his mother's folded wings. A snug little swan, I thought, littler than the others perhaps. A lucky little swan.

That night the wind came in from the north and the lake froze over. It stayed frozen. I wondered how they would manage. But I need not have worried. They swam about, keeping a pool of water near the island clear of ice. They had enough to eat, enough to drink. They would be fine. And every day the cygnets were growing. It was clear now that one of them was indeed much smaller, much weaker. But he was keeping up. He was coping. All was well.

Then, silently, as I slept one night, it snowed outside. It snowed on the farm, on the trees, on the frozen lake. I took bread crusts with me the next morning, just in case, and hurried down to the lake. As I came out of the woods, I saw the fox's paw prints in the snow. They were leading down toward the lake.

I was running, stumbling through the drifts, dreading all along what I might find.

The fox was stalking around the nest. My silver swan was standing her ground over her young, neck lowered in attack, her wings beating the air frantically, furiously. I shouted. I screamed. But I was too late and too far away to help.

Quick as a flash, the fox darted in, had her by the wing, and was dragging her away. I ran out onto the ice. I felt it crack and give suddenly beneath me. I was knee-deep in the lake then, still screaming, but the fox would not be put off. I could see the blood, red, bright red, on the snow. The five cygnets were scatter-ing in their terror. My silver swan was still fighting. But she was losing, and there was nothing I could do.

I heard the sudden singing of wings above me. The cob! The cob flying in, diving to attack. The fox took one look upward, released her victim, and scampered off over the ice, chased all the way by the cob.

For some moments I thought my silver swan was dead. She lay so still on the snow. But then she was on her feet and limping back to her island, one wing flapping feebly, the other trailing, covered in blood and useless. She was gathering her cygnets about her. They were all there. She was enfolding them, loving them, when the cob came flying back to her, landing awkwardly on the ice.

He stood over her all that day and would not leave her side. He knew she was dying. So, by then, did I. I had nothing but revenge and murder in my heart. Time and again, as I sat there at the lakeside, I thought of taking my father's gun and going into the woods to hunt down the killer fox. But then I would think of her kits and would know that she was only doing what a mother fox had to do.

For days I kept my cold, sad vigil by the lake. The cob was sheltering the cygnets now, my silver swan sleeping nearby, her head tucked under her wing. She scarcely ever moved.

I wasn't there, but I knew the precise moment she died. I knew it because she sang it. It's quite true what they say about

I heard the sudden singing of wings above me. The cob!

swans singing only when they die. I was at home. I had been sent out to fetch logs for the fire before I went up to bed. The world about me was crisp and bright under the moon. The song was clearer and sweeter than any human voice, than any birdsong, I had ever heard before. So sang my silver swan and died.

I expected to see her lying dead on the island the next morning. But she was not there. The cob was sitting still as a statue on his nest, his five cygnets around him.

I went looking for her. I picked up the trail of feathers and blood at the lakeside and followed where I knew it must lead, up through the woods. I approached silently. The fox kits were frolicking, fat and furry, in the sunshine, their mother close by, intent on her grooming. There was a terrible wreath of white feathers nearby, and telltale feathers, too, on her snout. She was trying to shake them off. How I hated her.

I ran at her. I picked up stones. I hurled them. I screamed at her. The foxes vanished into the undergrowth and left me alone in the woods. I picked up a silver feather and cried tears of such raw grief, such fierce anger.

Spring came at long last the next day and melted the ice. The cob and his five cygnets were safe. After that I came less and less to the lake. It wasn't quite the same without my silver swan. I went there only now and again, just to see how he was doing, how they were all doing.

At first, to my great relief, it seemed as if he was managing well enough on his own. Then one day I noticed there were only four cygnets swimming alongside him, the four bigger ones. I don't know what happened to the smaller one. He just wasn't there. Not so lucky, after all.

The cob would sometimes bring his cygnets to the lakeside to see me. I would feed them when he came, but then after a while he just stopped coming.

The weeks passed and the months passed, and the cygnets grew and flew. The cob scarcely left his island now. He stayed on the very spot I had last seen my silver swan. He did not swim; he did not feed; he did not preen himself. Day by day it became clearer that he was pining for her, dying for her.

Now my vigil at the lakeside was almost constant again. I had to be with him; I had to see him through. It was what my silver swan would have wanted, I thought.

So I was there when it happened. A swan flew in from nowhere one day, down onto the glassy stillness of the lake. She landed right in front of him. He walked down into the lake, settled into the water, and swam out to meet her. I watched them look each other over for just a few minutes. When they drank, they dipped their necks together, as one. When they flew, their wings beat together, as one.

Five years on and they're still together. Five years on and I still have the feather from my silver swan. I take it with me wherever I go. I always will. ✛

islands of inspiration

That story was inspired by the landscape of Scot-land, where I go to visit my younger brother. An island plays its part in it. I'm forever writing about islands; I love islands. I recently discov-ered a possible reason why. I learned that my very first nursery teacher in London had devised her own method of crowd control. To keep us from clambering on top of one another, she cut out small pieces of linoleum (one each) and whenever she wanted control, she sent us to our "islands." I must have loved even that island. She's got a lot to answer for!

Some years ago I was in New Zealand on a reading tour of schools and colleges. Bright-eyed and barefoot, the children in front of me were full of searching questions. One class had been reading a book of mine called *Why the Whales Came*. One small boy piped up: "You must have a really good imagination to have invented all those islands. Why did you call them Scilly? And how did you make up all those places and names, like Bryher and Samson, and Droppy Nose Point and Hell Bay and Popplestones and Sinking Porth and Rushy Bay?"

For just a moment I confess I considered lying to him. I longed to confirm his heart-warming opinion of me as some kind of imaginative genius. But I just couldn't do it. In the end I had to tell him that Scilly was in fact a real place, a scattering of little islands off the coast of Cornwall known as "the Fortunate Isles," that I had made nothing up except the story, and even some of that was true. A cloud of disappointment came over the upturned faces in front of me. Then I told them about Scilly, about the real place, and how I'd been on vacation there and discovered a place where every rock and wreck had a story to tell, many of them true stories, some apocryphal, perhaps, but all of them just waiting for me to steal them away and weave them into stories of my own.

Let me tell you about Scilly, because it's been very special to me. My wife, Clare, loved it as a child, loves it now. So do I. I remember the moment I first saw Scilly from the helicopter. A cluster of distant rocks lying in a translucent green sea, hurled there maybe by some defiant Cornish giant to sink a fleet of invading ships, or out of pique, perhaps, because someone had enraged him by climbing his bean stalk. The tide was way out that first time, so neither we nor our luggage could be off loaded at Bryher Quay. Instead we were landed on the rocks by Rushy Bay and had to be taken with our luggage in a wheelbarrow across the island to Marion and Keith Bennett's bed-and-breakfast cottage.

We spent the first couple of days exploring Bryher, our island—I was already feeling a kinship. The smallest of the five inhabited islands, you can walk around it from Green Bay to Rushy Bay to Droppy Nose Point, to Hell Bay, up through the "town" of twenty or so houses, in about an hour. But who was hurrying? Everywhere we stopped and simply stared. On one side of the island dunes and gently shelving soft white sand, the sea lapping listlessly; on the other the grim gray cliff faces of Hell Bay, where the sea surged and seethed, only wait- ing for the next storm, it seemed. We could have tea in Vine Café, ice cream for the children at Fraggle Rock, and a glass of wine on Green Bay as the sun set, watching the oyster- catchers taking off or a gig rowing up the Tresco channel.

I didn't want to leave Bryher at all, but Tresco and the Pentle Beach of Clare's childhood beckoned across the water. And there were boats going off to take visitors to see seals at the Eastern Rocks- —boats to St. Agnes, St. Martin's, and St. Mary's. We felt the need to explore. So we did. Tresco first. Pentle Beach was as long and as lovely as my wife remembered. We swam and swam in clear cold water, then we walked the length of it from the lushness of the Abbey Gardens to Cromwell's Castle, the sand whiter and finer than I'd ever imagined possible. We explored the ruined castle, walked through heather, lunched at the New Inn. Tresco is a more manicured place, tidier than Bryher, more beautiful perhaps, but less real as a living commu- nity, and so for me less appealing.

We went over to St. Agnes on a wild, wet day and ate the best pasties in the world at the Turks Head Inn overlooking the little harbor, before setting out over the island. The light- house that dominates the island is perhaps the handsomest building on Scilly, and out beyond it, as we came past the tiny school and the church, we saw Annet, where the puffins live and the hundreds of jagged rocks, some skulking just on or below the surface, waiting to ambush any unlucky or unwary ship that sails too close.

St. Martin's, the island out beyond uninhabited Teän (which had once been a leper colony), has a tiny school like St. Agnes—there's a bigger one on Tresco for the children of

both Bryher and Tresco—and a cricket pitch with unques-
tionably the best view in the entire world, looking out over the
sea toward the Eastern Isles and St. Mary's.

My first visit to St. Mary's after a week on the islands was a
shock. Cars! A bus! Even a policeman! But there was a fascinating museum that explained the history of Scilly from the
Bronze Age to the present day. Here I first learned that Scilly
had once been one large island, until a couple of thousand
years ago, when the sea broke through—a tsunami, perhaps
an earthquake—and made it into the archipelago of islands
and rocks we know today. Here I discovered how pirates had
come and pillaged and gone, how the Royal Navy had lost
two thousand men in one night when the fleet foundered on
the rocks in the eighteenth century, how Sir William Hamilton's
ship had gone down and all his treasures had been lost. Poor
man: he lost his wife, Emma, to Admiral Nelson, and then his
ship to the rugged rocks of Scilly. I learned too how Henry
VIII, then Oliver Cromwell, had built defenses around the
islands, and how it had been fortified later against Napoleon.
Flying boats came in here during the Second World War to
search the Atlantic for submarines. Scilly has always been a
far-flung outpost of defense.

And after every visit, there was the boat home to Bryher,
fast over the sun-dancing sea, or slower in the shallow chan-
nels gazing down to the seabed, or riding the huge waves out
by White Island, the boatman enjoying himself hugely at our
expense as we all did our best to hide our terror.

It was strange. On every other island I felt like a visitor.
Back on Bryher I felt I really belonged. I knew at once I was
going to write a story about this place, about the rugged and
robust people who lived there, who had lived there for cen-

turies before. But I had no idea what that story might be— until the second week of our vacation.

I needed a quiet place to work on a short story I was trying to write. "Samson is quiet," Marion said. "It's an uninhabited island. You'll just have rabbits and terns for company. We'll drop you off if you like."

So I found myself alone on Samson, an island of two hills covered in head-high bracken. On the beach I looked for the cowrie shells I was told I would find. I found no cowries, but I did see a peaty-black path leading up through the heather. I at once abandoned any resolve to finish my story. I would explore instead.

The path led me to a ruined cottage. No windows, no doors, no roof—just a chimney, four walls, and a fireplace. I found a broken clay pipe on the floor, a rusty knife, a scattered midden of limpet shells outside. I followed the track higher. If there was one cottage, there would be others, I reasoned. There were, and a well, too, in the middle of the island. I found myself at lunchtime in the highest and best-preserved cottage on the island. It was as I was sitting down eating my picnic by the granite fireplace that I felt for the first time that I was not alone. I heard footsteps outside. Rustling. I went to look. No one was there, yet there was someone. I could feel it. Eyes were watching me; I was quite sure of it. By the time Keith picked me up later in his boat, I was feeling very uncomfortable, indeed.

It was only on my return to Bryher that I learned how hunger and tragedy had driven the people from Samson one hundred and fifty years before, that there were stories of ghosts on Samson. I was not the first to feel their presence. I heard stories, too, of whales being washed up, of drowned sailors found on beaches during the First World War, of oppressive preventative officers—customs officials. A story was beginning to weave itself in my head. I wrote it before I came to Bryher the following year and called it *Why the Whales Came*. Within five years a film had been made. It was made on Bryher and starred Paul Scofield, Helen Mirren, David Suchet, and David Threlfall. And Gracie, one of the children in the story, was played by an island girl, Helen Pearce.

Shortly after filming, we discovered a leatherback turtle dead and gull-pecked on Samson, which sparked off the idea of my second Scilly book, *The Wreck of the Zanzibar*, a story of gigs and wrecks and the struggle to survive in the nineteenth century. Gigs play a huge part in this story, as indeed they do and have done in the life of Scilly. Wonderfully graceful, these seagoing rowing boats performed a vital role in the economy of the islands. Each island had (and still has) its own gig. The islanders would be on the lookout for sailing ships in need of pilots to navigate the treacherous waters of the English Channel. The first island gig to reach the ship got the job. This was lucrative work, too, much needed and sought after by each island. Gigs were also used, of course, to row out to wrecks, and often played a heroic part in rescuing sailors stranded at sea. One such dramatic rescue involved the Bryher gig that put to sea in a storm so violent that the gig couldn't be rowed out around Samson; so the crew had to carry her across the spit of the island before launching her again—an incident I used in *The Wreck of the Zanzibar*. But gigs were also used to go out to wrecks to claim them. An old Scilly prayer went something like this: "Dear God, we do not wish there to be a wreck, but if there has to be a wreck, then let it be near our island." Such wrecks must have brought some brief respite from the abject poverty and hunger Scillonians suffered in the days of the great sailing ships.

And the island gigs are rowed to this day: *Serica, Shah, Menavaur, Emperor, Golden Eagle,* and *Czar,* the Bryher gig. Every Friday night they race each other into St. Mary's, cheered on wildly by fiercely partisan tourists like me. Incidentally, why does *Czar* never win?

It was on a trip to the vegetable store on Bryher that I heard the story that triggered my third Scilly novel. The farmer who grew the vegetables had been plowing up his potato field when he came across a great hole in the ground. On close examination he discovered an ancient tomb. Inside were the remains of a fleece, a mirror, and a sword—the sword and mirror are now in the museum of St. Mary's. Experts who examined it declared the tomb to be about two thousand years old. Scilly is littered with ancient tombs— I've lain in one on Samson Hill. It fits me perfectly! It so happened that I had already written my version of the King Arthur story, *Arthur, High King of Britain*—the only genuine autobiography—and had set his resting place on Scilly in a cave under an island called Little Arthur, one of the Eastern Isles. So this new discovery of the ancient tomb in the potato field on Bryher had to be Sir Bedevere's tomb, I thought, and the sword Excalibur, of course. He never threw Excalibur back in the lake as the wounded King Arthur had instructed him. Bedevere didn't want to see Camelot die, so, unbeknownst to the king, he kept Excalibur, the talisman of Camelot's power, to be ready for Arthur when the time came to use it again. Well, that's my story and I'm sticking to it. Anyway, it's the story behind my book *The Sleeping Sword.*

I'm looking forward to my next summer in Marion's cottage, the same cottage we always have. The hospitality will be as warm, the beaches as clean as the sea. The fog will roll in and hide us from the rest of the world. Then there'll be a wind, and the sea will dance with light again. But either way, whatever the weather, I will feel a perfect peace. I will feel at home. And who knows what will turn up this time? All I know is that something will. On islands, something always does.

Robert Louis Stevenson loved islands, too—Scottish ones, Pacific ones, he wasn't fussy. He wrote the greatest island book of all time. As I've said, if there's one book that fired my imagination as a young boy, it was *Treasure Island.*

I think I first heard of Stevenson and *Treasure Island* through a card game I used to play called Author. The object was to match up cards to make a sort of literary Happy Families—the author's name being the family name, the author's book titles the members of the family. It's how I first learned, for instance, that Nathaniel Hawthorne wrote *The Scarlet Letter,* that Charles Dickens wrote not only *A Christmas Carol* but *David Copperfield* too, that Thackeray's middle name was Makepeace, and, most importantly, that Robert Louis Stevenson wrote *The Strange Case of Dr. Jekyll and Mr. Hyde, Kidnapped, Catriona,* and *Treasure Island.*

I longed to collect the Stevenson cards because I loved to look into his face—the authors' faces were the link on all the cards. Stevenson's hair was long and lank, his face thin and pale, his eyes thoughtful, kind, and intelligent. He was everything I longed to be, but couldn't—I was round-faced, red-faced, with jug ears and sticky-up short hair, and of only average intelligence. Whenever I looked into his eyes, I felt he was looking back at me, that he was in some way genuinely interested in me, that perhaps he thought of me as a kindred spirit.

So, to collect the Stevenson cards before anyone else was always my main ambition. The other authors I cared less about (though I still wanted to win). I never cared much for Dickens, who looked like a tired bloodhound with a beard! No, Robert Louis Stevenson was the one for me; he was my kind of man. When later on I'd read all his extraordinary books, and when I'd read something of his life—of his adventures and travels, his fame, his last island home, and his tragic early death— there stirred in me the longing to follow in his footsteps, to fol- low where my dreams led me, to dare all—even to die young if I had to. But that was many years ago, and I've long since grown out of that last romantic aspiration. However, the excite- ment I found in his stories and my admiration for Stevenson as a writer and a man have stayed with me all my life.

So what exactly is the magic of Stevenson's genius as a writer and storyteller? For a story to resonate, to captivate the reader, a writer has to make the unbelievable believable. The reader must believe absolutely in the characters and their rela- tionships, in the place and time in which the story happens. The unfolding of the plot must also be entirely credible, not contrived, but growing organically out of circumstance.

With a deft dab of description, with a turn of phrase or a tone of voice, Robert Louis Stevenson brings his characters in *Treasure Island* to life: Jim Hawkins, Long John Silver, Dr. Livesey, Ben Gunn, and the rest. Each is both plausible and complex. Through Jim's wide eyes, we see the Jekyll and Hyde in Long John Silver. Like Jim, we are at first entertained and entranced by Silver, then appalled and entranced again. The thread of the story is seamless because no one is pulling strings except the characters themselves—the author just goes along with them, or so it seems. It is all made so real for us, so convincing, that we believe at once in poor marooned Ben Gunn; live with Jim as he witnesses murder; feel the danger, the tension, and the companionship behind the stockade on Treasure Island.

As for place, I *know* the Admiral Benbow Inn, where the book begins, as well as I do my own village pub. I can picture every nook and cranny of it. I *know* the *Hispaniola* as well as if I'd sailed on her—from the exact location of the barrel of apples in which Jim hides to how the sails are set and how the lantern swings below in the cabin. And Treasure Island I know as well as I know the island of Bryher, because Jim Hawkins has taken me to the island and shown me the lie of the land, the marshy groves, the stockade on the hill. I know the entire coastline as Jim takes the helm of the *Hispaniola* and single-handedly beaches the ship. All utterly incredible, but made credible.

Then there's the plot itself. From the first time we hear the eerie refrain "Fifteen men on the dead man's chest—Yo-ho-ho, and a bottle of rum!" and then learn of the mysterious "black spot," we are hooked. And once hooked, Stevenson never lets us go. He takes us on a giddy journey of twists and turns of fate, through hope to horror and despair, and back to hope again—all of it unexpected, all of it thrilling. He pulls no punches—there is violence and blood. These are no cardboard cutout pirates—these are cut*throat* pirates. We see man's greed for gold in the raw. We see men murdered, watch them die, hear their screams. We live the adventure with Jim, are terrified with him, and all the while we are urging him on, willing him to watch out, to win through somehow.

Read the book. If you haven't already, you have a treat in

store. If you've read it before, then do it again. It will surprise and excite you all over again. I've just reread it for the umpteenth time in my life and was enthralled, just as I was all those years ago as a young boy.

I do have one thing, though, that I hold against Stevenson: he wrote *Treasure Island* and I didn't. It's the one book I should love to have written myself. But I suppose it's just as well, because although I hope I might have told the tale well enough, Stevenson told it wonderfully, beautifully, poeti-cally. For Stevenson wasn't just a fine storyteller—he was one of the greatest writers, and to my mind, *Treasure Island* is the most masterly of his master-pieces. ⸺

the mozart question

The question I am most often asked is always easy enough to answer. Question: how did you get started as a writer? Answer: strangely enough, by asking someone almost exactly that very same question, which I was only able to ask in the first place by receiving a dose of extraordinarily good fortune.

I had better explain.

My good fortune was, of course, someone else's rotten luck — it is often that way, I find. The phone call sounded distraught. It came on a Sunday evening. I had only been working at the paper for three weeks. I was a cub reporter, this, my first paid job.

"Lesley?" It was my boss, chief arts correspondent Meryl Monkton, a lady not to be messed with. She did not waste time with niceties; she never did. "Listen, Lesley, I have a problem. I was due to go to Venice tomorrow to interview Paolo Levi."

"Paolo Levi?" I asked. "The violinist?"

"Is there any other Paolo Levi?" She did not try to hide her irritation. "Now, look, Lesley. I've had an accident, a skiing accident, and I'm stuck in a hospital in Switzerland. You'll have to go to Venice instead of me."

"Oh, that's terrible," I said, smothering as best I could the excitement surging inside me. Three weeks into the job, and I'd be interviewing the great Paolo Levi, and in Venice!

Talk about her accident, I told myself. *Sound concerned. Sound very concerned.*

"How did it happen?" I asked. "The skiing accident, I mean."

"Skiing," she snapped. "If there's one thing I can't abide, Lesley, it's people feeling sorry for me."

"Sorry," I said.

"I would postpone it if I could, Lesley," she went on, "but I just don't dare. It's taken me more than a year to persuade him to do it. It'll be his first interview in years. And even then I had to agree not to ask him the Mozart question. So don't ask him the Mozart question, is that clear? If you do, he'll likely cancel the whole interview—he's done it before. We're really lucky to get him, Lesley. I only wish I could be there to do it myself. But you'll have to do."

"The Mozart question?" I asked rather tentatively.

The silence at the end of the phone was long.

"You mean to say you don't know about Paolo Levi and the Mozart question? Where have you been, girl? Don't you know anything at all about Paolo Levi?"

I suddenly felt I might lose the opportunity altogether if I did not immediately sound informed, and well informed, too.

"Well, he would have been born sometime in the mid-1950s," I began. "He must be about fifty by now."

"Exactly fifty in two weeks' time," Meryl Monkton interrupted wearily. "His London concert is his fiftieth birthday concert. That's the whole point of the interview. Go on."

I rattled off all I knew. "Child prodigy and genius, like Yehudi Menuhin. Played his first major concert when he was thirteen. Probably best known for his playing of Bach and Vivaldi. Like Menuhin, he played often with Grappelli, equally at home with jazz or Scottish fiddle music or Beethoven. Has played in practically every major concert hall in the world, in front of presidents and kings and queens. I heard him at the Royal Festival Hall in London, five years ago, I think. He was playing Beethoven's Violin Concerto; he was wonderful. Doesn't like applause. Never waits for applause. Doesn't believe in it, apparently. The night I saw him, he just walked off the stage and didn't come back. He thinks it's the music that should be applauded, if anything, or perhaps the composer, but certainly not the musician. Says that the silence after the performance is part of the music and should not be interrupted. Doesn't record, either. Believes music should be live, not canned. Protects his privacy fiercely. Solitary. Reticent. Lives alone in Venice, where he was born. Just about the most famous musician on the planet, and—"

"*The* most famous, Lesley, but he hates obsequiousness. He likes to be talked to straight. So no bowing or scraping, no wide-eyed wonder, and above all, no nerves. Can you do that?"

"Yes, Meryl," I replied, knowing only too well that I would have the greatest difficulty even finding my voice in front of the great man.

"And whatever you do, stick to the music. He'll talk till the cows come home about music and composers. But no personal stuff. And at all costs, keep off the Mozart question. Oh, yes, and don't take a tape recorder with you. He hates gadgets. Only shorthand. You *can* do shorthand, I suppose? Three thousand words. It's your big chance, so don't mess it up, Lesley."

No pressure, then, I thought.

*   *   *

So there I was the next evening outside Paolo Levi's apartment in the Dorsoduro in Venice, on the dot of six o'clock, my throat dry, my heart pounding, trying to compose myself. It occurred to me again, as it had often on the plane, that I still had no idea what this Mozart question was, only that I mustn't ask it. The night air was cold, the kind of cruel chill that seeps instantly into your bones, deep into your kidneys, and makes your ears ache. This didn't seem to bother the street performers in the square behind me: several grotesquely masked figures on stilts strutting across the square, and an entirely silver statue-man posing immobile outside the café with a gaggle of tourists gazing wonderingly at him.

The door opened, and there he was in front of me, Paolo Levi, neat, trim, his famous hair long to his shoulders and jet black.

"I'm Lesley McInley," I said. "I've come from London."

"From the newspaper, I suppose." There was no welcoming smile. "You'd better come in. Shut the door behind you; I hate the cold." His English was perfect, not a trace of an accent. He seemed to be able to follow my thoughts. "I speak English quite well," he said as we went up the stairs. "Language is like music. You learn it best through listening."

He led me down a hallway and into a large room, empty except for a couch by the window piled high with cushions at one end, a grand piano in the center, and a music stand nearby. At the other end were just two armchairs and a table. Nothing else. "I like to keep it empty," he said.

It was uncanny. He *was* reading my thoughts. Now I felt even more unnerved.

"Sound needs space to breathe, just the same as we need air," he said.

He waved me to a chair and sat down. "You'll have some mint tea?" he said, pouring me a cup. His dark blue cardigan and gray corduroy trousers were somehow both shabby and elegant at the same time. The bedroom slippers he wore looked incongruous but comfortable. "My feet, they hate the cold more than the rest of me." He was scrutinizing me now, his eyes sharp and shining. "You're younger than I expected," he said. "Twenty-three?" He didn't wait to have his estimate confirmed—he knew he was right, and he was. "You have heard me play?"

"Beethoven's Violin Concerto. The Royal Festival Hall in London, a few years ago. I was a student." I noticed his violin then, and his bow, on the window ledge.

"I like to practice by the window," he said, "so I can watch the world go by on the canal. It passes the time. Even as a child, I never liked practicing much. And I love to be near water, to look out on it. When I go to London, I have to have a room by the Thames. In Paris I must be by the Seine. I love the light that water makes." He sipped his mint tea, his eyes never leaving me. "Shouldn't you be asking me questions?" He went on. "I'm talk-ing too much. Journalists always make me nervous. I talk too much when I'm nervous. When I go to the dentist's, I talk. Before a concert I talk. So let's get this over with, shall we? And not too many questions, please. Why don't we keep it simple? You ask me one question and then let me ramble on. Shall we try that?" I didn't feel at all that he was being dismissive or patroniz-ing, just straight. That didn't make it any easier, though.

I had done my research, made pages of notes, prepared dozens of questions; but now, under his expectant gaze, I simply could not gather my thoughts.

"Well, I know I can't ask you the Mozart question, Signor Levi," I began, "because I've been told not to. I don't even know what the Mozart question is, so I couldn't ask it even if I wanted to, and anyway, I know you don't like it, so I won't."

With every blundering word, I was digging myself into a deeper hole. In my desperation, I blurted out the first question that came into my head.

"Signor Levi," I said, "I wonder if you'd mind telling me

singing for mrs. pettigrew

how you got started. I mean, what made you pick up a violin and play that first time?" It was such an obvious question, and personal, too, just the kind of question I shouldn't have asked.

His reaction only confirmed that. He sat back in his chair and closed his eyes. For fully a couple of minutes, he said nothing. I was quite sure he was trying to control his impatience, his rage even, that he was going to open his eyes and ask me to leave at once. When he did open his eyes, he simply stared up at the ceiling for a while. I could see from the seriousness of his whole demeanor that he was making a decision, and I feared the worst. But instead of throwing me out, he stood up and walked slowly to the couch by the window. He picked up his violin and sat back on the cushions with his violin resting on his drawn-up knees. He plucked a string or two and tuned it.

"I will tell you a story," he began. "After it is over, you will need to ask me no more questions. Someone once told me that all secrets are lies. The time has come, I think, not to lie anymore."

He paused. I felt he was stiffening his resolve, gathering his strength.

"I will start with my father. Papa was a barber. He kept a little barbershop just behind the Accademia, near the bridge, two minutes from here. We lived above the shop, Mama, Papa, and I, but I spent most of my time downstairs in the barbershop, sitting on the chairs and swinging my legs, smiling at him and his customers in the mirror, and just watching him. I loved those days. I loved him. At the time of these memories, I must have been about nine years old. Small for my age. I always was. I still am."

He spoke slowly, very deliberately, as if he were living it again, seeing again everything he was telling me. My shorthand was quick and automatic, so I had time to look up at him occasionally as he spoke. I sensed right away that I was the first person ever to hear this story, so I knew even as he told it just how momentous the telling of it was for him, and in a totally different way it was for me, too.

"Papa was infinitely deft with his fingers, his scissors playing a constantly changing tune. It seemed to me like a new improvisation for every customer, the snipping unhesitatingly skillful, so fast that it was mesmerizing. He would work always in complete silence, conducting the music of his scissors with his comb. His customers knew better than to interrupt the performance, and so did I. I think perhaps I must have known his customers almost as well as he did. I grew up with them. They were all regulars. Some would close their eyes as Papa worked his magic; others would look back in the mirror at me and wink.

"Shaving was just as fascinating to me, just as rhythmical, too: the swift sweep and dab of the brush, the swish and slap of the razor as Papa sharpened it on the strap, then each time the miraculous unmasking as he stroked the foam away to reveal a recognizable face once more.

"After it was all over, he and his customers did talk, and all the banter among them was about soccer, Inter Milan in particu-lar, or sometimes the machinations of politicians and women. What they said I cannot exactly remember, probably because I couldn't understand most of it, but I do know they laughed a lot. I do remember that. Then the next customer would take his seat, and a new silence would descend before the performance started again and the music of the scissors began. I am sure I first learned about rhythm in that barbershop, and about concentration. I learned to listen, too.

"Papa wasn't just the best barber in all of Venice—everyone said that—he was a musician, too, a violinist. But strangely he was a violinist who never played the violin. I never heard him play, not once. I only knew he was a violinist because Mama had told me so. She had tears in her eyes whenever she told me about it. That surprised me, because she was not a crying woman. He had been so brilliant as a violinist, the best in the whole orchestra, she said. When I asked why he didn't play anymore, she turned away from me, went very quiet, and told me I'd have to ask Papa myself. So I did. I asked him time and again, and each time he would simply shrug and say something meaningless like: 'People change, Paolo. Times change.' And that would be that.

"Papa was never a great talker at the best of times, even at home, but I could tell that in this case he was hiding something, that he found my questions both irksome and intrusive. That didn't stop me. I kept at him. Every time he refused to talk about it, I became more suspicious, more sure he had something to hide. It was a child's intuition, I suppose. I sensed a deep secret, but I also sensed after a while that Papa was quite unmovable, that if I were ever going to unlock the secret, it would be Mama who would tell me.

"As it turned out, my instinct was right. In the end, my almost perpetual pestering proved fruitful, and Mama capitulated — but not in a way I had expected. 'All right, Paolo,' she said after I'd been nagging her about it unmercifully one morning. 'If I show you the violin, will you promise me you'll stop asking your wretched questions? And you're never, ever to tell Papa I showed you. He'd be very angry. Promise me now.'

"So I promised, promised faithfully, and then stood in their bedroom and watched as she climbed up on a chair to get it down from where it had been hidden on top of the cupboard. It was wrapped up in an old gray blanket. I kneeled on the bed beside her as she pulled away the blanket and opened the violin case. I remember it smelled musty. The maroon lining inside was faded and worn to tatters. Mama picked up the violin with infinite care, reverently almost. Then she handed it to me.

"I stroked the polished grain of the wood, which was the color of honey, dark honey on the front, and golden honey underneath. I ran my fingers along the black pegs, the mottled bridge, the exquisitely carved scroll. It was so light to hold, I remember. I wondered at its fragile beauty. I knew at once that all the music in the world was hidden away inside this violin, yearning to come out. I longed to be the one to let it out, to rest it under my chin, to play the strings, to try the bow. I wanted there and then to bring it to life, to have it sing for me, to hear all the music we could make together. But when I asked if I could play it, Mama took a sudden fright and said Papa might hear down below in the barbershop and he'd be furious with her for showing it to me, that he never wanted it to be played again. He hadn't so much as looked at it in years. When I asked why, she reminded me of my promise not to ask any more questions. She almost snatched the violin away from me, laid it back in its case, wrapped it again in the blanket, and put it back up on top of the cupboard.

"'You don't know it exists, Paolo. You never saw it, understand? And from now on I don't want to hear another word about it, all right? You promised me, Paolo.'

"I suppose seeing Papa's old violin, holding it as I had, marveling at it must have satisfied my curiosity for a while, because I kept my promise. Then late one summer's evening, I was lying half awake in my bed when I heard the sound of a violin. I thought Papa must have changed his mind and was playing again at last. But then I heard him and Mama talking in the kitchen below and realized that the music was coming from much farther away.

"I listened at the window. I could hear it only intermittently over the sound of people talking and walking, over the throbbing engines of passing water taxis, but I was quite sure now that it was coming from somewhere beyond the bridge. I had to find out. In my pajamas I stole past the kitchen door, down the stairs, and out into the street. It was a warm night and quite dark. I ran up over the bridge, and there, all on his own, standing by a wall in the square, was an old man playing the violin.

"No one else was there. No one had stopped to listen. I squatted

He was so wrapped up in his playing that he did not notice me at first.

down as close as I dared. He was so wrapped up in his playing that he did not notice me at first. I could see now that he was much older than Papa. Then he saw me crouching there, watching him. He stopped playing. 'Hello,' he said. 'You're out late. What's your name?' He had kind eyes; I noticed that at once.

"'Paolo,' I told him. 'Paolo Levi. My papa plays the violin. He played in an orchestra once.'

"'So did I,' said the old man, 'all my life. But now I am what I always wanted to be, a soloist. I shall play you some Mozart. Do you like Mozart?'

"'I don't know,' I replied. I knew Mozart's name, of course, but I don't think I had ever listened to any of his music.

"'He wrote this piece when he was even younger than you. I should guess that you're about seven.'

"'Nine,' I said.

"'Well, Mozart wrote this when he was just six years old. He wrote it for the piano, but I can play it on the violin.'

"So he played Mozart, and I listened. As he played, others came and gathered around for a while before dropping a coin or two in his violin case and moving on. I didn't move on. I stayed. The music he played to me that night touched my soul. It was the night that changed my life forever.

"Whenever I crossed the Accademia Bridge after that, I always looked for him. Whenever I heard him playing, I went to listen. I never told Mama or Papa. I think it was the first secret I kept from them. But I did not feel guilty about it, not one bit. After all, hadn't they kept a secret from me? Then one evening the old man—I had found out by now that his name was Benjamin Horowitz and that he was sixty-two years old—one evening he let me hold his violin, showing me how to hold it properly, how to draw the bow across the strings, how to make it sing. The moment I did that, I knew I had to be a violinist. I have never wanted to do or be anything else since.

"So Benjamin—Signor Horowitz, I always called him then—became my first teacher. Now every time I ran over the bridge to see him, he would show me a little more, how to tighten the bow just right, how to use the resin, how to hold the violin under my chin using no hands at all, and what each string was called. That was when I told him about Papa's violin at home, and about how he didn't play it anymore. 'He couldn't anyway,' I said, 'because it's a bit broken. I think it needs mending. Two of the strings are missing, the A and the E, and there's hardly a hair left on the bow at all. But I could practice on it if it was mended, couldn't I?'

"'Bring it to my house sometime,' Benjamin said, 'and leave it with me. I'll see what I can do.'

"It wasn't difficult to escape unnoticed. I just waited until after school. Mama was still at the laundry around the corner in Rio de le Romite, where she worked. Papa was downstairs with his customers. To reach the violin on top of the cupboard, I had to put a suitcase on the chair and then climb up. It wasn't easy, but I managed. I ran through the streets hugging it to me. From the Dorsoduro to the Arsenale, where Benjamin lived, is not that far if you know the way—nowhere is that far in Venice—and I knew the way quite well, because my aunt Sophia lived there and we visited her often. All I had to do was find Benjamin's street. I had to ask for help, but I found it.

"Benjamin lived up a narrow flight of stairs in one small room with a bed in one corner and a basin in the other. On the wall were lots of concert posters. 'Some of the concerts I played,' he said. 'Milan, London, New York. Wonderful places, won- derful people, wonderful music. It is a wonderful world out there. There are times when it can be hard to go on believing that. But always believe it, Paolo, because it is true. And music helps to make it so. Now, show me that violin of yours.'

"He studied it closely, holding it up to the light, tapping it. 'A very fine instrument,' he said. 'You say this belongs to your father?'

"'And now I want to play it myself,' I told him.

"'It's a bit on the large side for a young lad like you,' he said, tucking the violin under my chin and stretching my arm to see how far I could reach. 'But a big violin is better than no violin at all. You'll manage. You'll grow into it.'

"'And when it's mended, will you teach me?' I asked him. 'I've got lots of money saved up from my sweeping; so many *lire* they cover all my bed when I spread them out, from the end of the bed right up to my pillow.'

"He laughed at that and told me he would teach me for nothing because I was his best listener, his lucky mascot. 'When you're not there,' he said, 'everyone walks by, and my violin case stays empty. Then you come along and sit there. That's when they always stop to listen, and that's when they leave their money. So a lesson or two will just be paying you back, Paolo. I'll have the violin ready as soon as I can, and then we can start your lessons.'

"It was a week or two before the violin was mended. I dreaded that Mama or Papa might discover it was missing. But my luck held, and they didn't, and my lessons began. Whenever I wasn't having my lessons with Benjamin, Papa's violin, now restrung and restored, lay in its case wrapped in the gray blanket and hid-den away on top of their bedroom cupboard. My secret was safe, I thought. But secrets are never safe, however well hidden. Sooner or later the truth will come out, and in this case it was to be sooner rather than later.

"I took to the violin as if it had been a limb I had been miss-ing all my life. I seemed to be able to pick up everything Benjamin taught me, effortlessly and instinctively. Under his kind tutelage, my confidence simply burgeoned, my playing blossomed. I found I could make my violin—Papa's violin, rather—sing with the voice of an angel. Benjamin and I felt the excitement and pleasure of my progress as keenly as each other. 'I think this instrument was invented just for you, Paolo,' he told me one day. 'Or maybe you were made for it. Either way, it is a perfect match.' I loved every precious moment of my lessons and always dreaded their ending. We would finish every lesson with a cup of mint tea made with fresh mint. I loved it. Ever since, I have always treated myself to a cup of mint tea after practice. It's something I always look forward to.

"I remember one day, with the lesson over, we were drinking tea at his table when he looked across at me, suddenly very seri-ous. 'It is strange, Paolo,' he said, 'but as I was watching you playing a moment ago, I felt I had known you before, a long, long time ago. And then just now I thought about your name, Levi. It is a common enough name, I know, but his name was Levi, too. It is him you remind me of. I am sure of it. He was the youngest player in our orchestra, no more than a boy, really. Gino, he was called.'

"'But my father is named Gino,' I told him. 'Maybe it was him. Maybe you played with my father. Maybe you know him.'

"'It can't be possible,' Benjamin breathed. He was staring at me now as if I were a ghost. 'No, it can't be. The Gino Levi I knew must be dead, I am sure of it. I have not heard of him in a long while, a very long while. But you never know, I suppose. Maybe I should meet your papa, and your mama, too. It's about time, anyway. You've been coming for lessons for over six months now. They need to know they have a wonderful violinist for a son.'

"'No, you can't!' I cried. 'He'd find out! You can't tell him. You mustn't!' Then I told him, through my tears, all my secret, about how Mama had shown me Papa's violin and made me promise never to say anything, never to tell Papa, and how I'd kept it a secret all this while, mending the violin, the lessons, everything.

"'Secrets, Paolo,' said Benjamin, 'are lies by another name.

You do not lie to those you love. A son should not hide things from his papa and his mama. You must tell them your secret, Paolo. If you want to go on playing the violin, you will have to tell them. If you want me to go on teaching you, you will have to tell them. And now is usually a good time to do what must be done, particularly when you don't want to do it.'

"'Will you come with me?' I begged him. 'I can only do it if you come with me.'

"'If you like,' he said, smiling.

"Benjamin carried Papa's violin for me that day, and held my hand all the way back to the Dorsoduro. I dreaded having to make my confession. I knew how hurt they would be. All the way I rehearsed what I was going to say over and over again. Mama and Papa were upstairs in the kitchen when we came in. I introduced Benjamin and then, before anyone had a chance to say anything, before I lost my courage entirely, I launched at once into my prepared confession, how I hadn't really stolen Papa's violin, just borrowed it to get it mended and to practice on. But that's as far as I got. To my surprise, they were not looking angry. In fact, they weren't looking at me at all. They were just staring up at Benjamin as if quite unable to speak. Benjamin spoke before they did. 'Your mama and papa and I, I think perhaps we do know one another,' he said. 'We played together once, did we not? Don't you remember me, Gino?'

" 'Benjamin?' As Papa started to his feet, the chair went over behind him.

" 'And if I am not much mistaken, Signora,' Benjamin went on, looking now at Mama, 'you must be little Laura Adler—all of us violins, all of us there, and all of us still here. It is like a miracle. It *is* a miracle.'

"What happened next I can see as if it were yesterday. It was suddenly as if I were not in the room at all. The three of them seemed to fill the kitchen, arms around each other, and crying openly, crying through their laughter. I stood there mystified, trying to piece together all I had heard, all that was going on before my eyes. Mama played the violin, too! She had never told me that!

" 'You see, Paolo,' said Benjamin, smiling down at me, 'didn't I tell you once it was a wonderful world? Twenty years. It's been twenty years or more since I last saw your mama and papa. I had no idea they were still alive. I always hoped they survived, hoped they were together, these two young lovebirds, but I never believed it, not really.'

"Mama was drying her eyes on her apron. Papa was so overcome, he couldn't speak. They sat down then, hands joined around the table as if unwilling to let each other go for fear this reunion might turn out to be no more than a dream.

"Benjamin was the first to recover. 'Paolo was about to tell you something, I think,' he said. 'Weren't you, Paolo?' I told them everything then: how I'd gone for my lessons, how Benjamin had been the best teacher in all the world. I dared to look up only when I'd finished. Instead of the disapproval and disappoint-ment I had expected, both Mama and Papa were simply glowing with joy and pride.

"'Didn't I say Paolo would tell us, Papa?' she said. 'Didn't I tell you we should trust him? You see, Paolo, I often take down my violin, just to touch it, to look at it. Papa doesn't like me to, but I do it all the same, because this violin is my oldest friend. Papa forgives me, because he knows I love this violin, that it is a part of me. You remember I showed it to you that day, Paolo? It wasn't long after that it went missing, was it? I knew it had to be you. Then it came back, mended miraculously. And after school you were never home, and when you weren't home, the violin was always gone, too. I told Papa, didn't I, Papa? I told him you'd tell us when you were ready. We put two and two together; we thought you might be practicing somewhere, but it never occurred to us that you were having lessons, nor that you had a

teacher—and certainly not that your teacher was Benjamin
Horowitz, who taught us and looked after us like a father all
those years ago.' She cried again then, her head on Papa's
shoulder.

"'But you told me it was Papa's violin, that he'd put it away
and never wanted to play it again, ever,' I said.

"At this, the three of them looked at one another. I knew then
that they all shared the same secret, and that without a word passing between them they were deciding whether they should reveal
it, if this was the right moment to tell me. I often wondered later
whether, if Benjamin had not come that day, they would ever
have told me. As it was, they looked to Papa for the final decision,
and it was he who invited me to the table to join them. I think I
knew then, even before Papa began, that I was in some way part
of their secret.

"'Mama and I,' Papa began, 'we try never to speak of this,
because the memories we have are like nightmares, and we want
to forget. But you told us your secret. There is a time for truth, it
seems, and it has come. Truth for truth, maybe.'

"So began the saddest, yet the happiest story I ever heard.
When the story became too painful, as it often did, they passed
it from one to the other, so that all three shared it. I listened,

horrified, at the same time honored that they trusted me enough with their story, the story of their lives. Each told their part with great care, explaining as they went along so that I would under‑ stand, because I was a boy of nine who knew very little then of the wickedness of the world. I wish I could remember their exact words, but I can't, so I won't even try. I'll just tell you their story my own way, about how they lived together, how they nearly died together, and how they were saved by music.

"The three of them were brought by train to a concentration camp, from all over Europe: Benjamin from Paris, Mama from Warsaw, Papa from here, from Venice; all musicians, all Jewish, and all bound for the gas chamber and extermination like so many millions. They survived only because they were all able to say yes to one question put to them by an SS officer on arrival at the camp. 'Is there anyone among you who can play an orchestral instrument, who is a professional musician?' They did not know when they stepped forward that they would at once be separated from their families, would have to watch them being herded off toward those hellish chimneys, never to be seen again.

"There were auditions, of course, and by now they knew they were playing for their lives. There were rehearsals then, and it was during these rehearsals that the three of them met. Benjamin was a good twenty years older than Mama and Papa, who were very much the babies of the orchestra, both of them just twenty. Why the orchestra was rehearsing, whom they would be playing for, they did not know and they did not ask. To ask was to draw attention to oneself. This they knew was not the way to survive, and in the camp, to survive was everything. They played Mozart, a lot of Mozart. The repertoire was for the most part light and happy—*Eine kleine Nachtmusik,* the Clarinet Concerto in A major, minuets, dances, marches. And Strauss was popular, too— waltzes, always waltzes. Playing was very hard, because their fingers were so cold that sometimes they could hardly feel them, because they were weak with hunger and frequently sick. Sick- ness had to be hidden, because sickness, once discovered, would mean death. The SS men were always there watching, and everyone knew, too, what awaited them if they did not play well enough.

"At first they gave concerts only for the SS officers. Papa said you just had to pretend they were not there. You simply lost yourself in the music—it was the only way. Even when they applauded, you did not look up. You never looked them in the eye. You played with total commitment. Every performance was your best performance, not to please them, but to show them what you could do, to prove to them how good you were despite all they were doing to humiliate you, to destroy you in body and soul. 'We fought back with our music,' Papa said. 'It was our only weapon.'

"Papa could speak no Polish, Mama no Italian, but their eyes met as they were playing—as often as possible, Mama said. To begin with, it might have been their shared joy in music-making, but very soon they knew they loved each other. The whole orchestra knew it, even before they did, Benjamin told me. 'Our little lovebirds' they were called. For everyone else in the orchestra, he said, they represented a symbol of hope for the future; and so they were much loved, much protected. For Mama and Papa, their love numbed the pain and was a blessed refuge from the constant fear they were living through, from the horror of all that was going on around them.

"But there was among them a shared shame. They were being fed when others were not. They were being kept alive while others went to the gas chamber. Many were consumed by guilt, and this guilt was multiplied a thousand times when they discovered the real reason the orchestra had been assembled, why they had been rehearsing all this time. The concerts for the SS officers turned out to be sinister dress rehearsals for something a great deal worse.

"One cold morning with snow on the ground, they were made to assemble out in the compound with their instruments and ordered to sit down and play close to the camp gates. Then the train arrived, the cars packed with new prisoners. Once the prisoners were all out, they were lined up and then divided. The old and young and the frail were herded past the orchestra on their way, they were told, to the shower block; the able-bodied, those fit for work, were taken off toward the huts. And all the while, Mama and Papa and Benjamin and the others played their Mozart. They all understood soon enough what it was for—to calm the terror, to beguile each new trainload into a false sense of security. They were part of a deadly sham. They knew well enough that the shower block was a gas chamber.

"Week after week they played, month after month, train after train. And twenty-four hours a day, the chimneys of the crematorium spewed out their fire and their smoke and their stench. Until there were no more trains, until the day the camps were liberated. This was the last day Benjamin ever remembered seeing Mama and Papa. They were all terribly emaciated by now, he said, and looked unlikely to survive. But they had. Mama and Papa had walked together out of the camp. They had played duets for bread and shelter, all across Europe. They were still playing to survive.

"When at last they got home to Venice, Papa smashed his violin and burned it, vowing never to play music again. But Mama kept hers. She thought of it as her talisman, her savior and her friend, and she would neither sell it nor abandon it. She said it had brought her through all the horrors of the camp, brought them safely across Europe, back to Papa's home in Venice. It had saved their lives.

"Papa kept his vow. He never played a note of music again. After all that had happened, he could hardly bear to hear it, which is why Mama had not played her violin, either, in all these years. But she would not be parted from it and had kept it safe at the top of their bedroom cupboard, hoping against hope, she said, that one day Papa might change his mind and be able to love music again and even play it. He never had. But they had survived, and they were in time blessed with a child, a boy they called Paolo—a happy ending, Benjamin said. And I was the one who had brought the three of them together again, he said. So two happy endings.

"As for Benjamin, he had found his way back to Paris after a while, and played again in his old orchestra. He had married a French woman, Françoise, a cellist who had died only recently. He had come to Venice because he had always loved visiting the

city and always longed to live looking out over water, and because
Vivaldi was born here—he had always loved Vivaldi above all
other composers. He played in the streets not just for the money,
though that was a help, but because he could not bear not to play
his violin. And he loved playing solo violin at last. He was more
like Mama, he said. It was music that had kept him alive in the
camp, and music had been his constant companion ever since.
He could not imagine living a single day of his life without it,
which was why, he said, he would dearly like to go on teaching
me, if Mama and Papa would allow it.

"'Does he play well, Benjamin?' Mama asked. 'Can we hear
him, Papa? Please.'

"Papa, I could see, was struggling with himself. 'So long as
it's not Mozart,' he said finally. So I played the Winter concerto
from Vivaldi's *Four Seasons,* Benjamin's favorite piece. Papa sat
listening with closed eyes throughout.

"When I had finished, Benjamin said, 'Well, Gino, what do
you think? He has a great and wonderful talent, your son, a rare
gift you have both given him.'

"'Then it must not be wasted,' said Papa quietly.

"So every day without fail after that, I went for my violin lessons with Benjamin in his little apartment in the Arsenale. Papa

could not bring himself to listen to me playing, but sometimes Mama came along with me and sat and listened, and afterward she always hugged me so tight it hurt, but I did not mind, not one bit. I began to play in the streets alongside Benjamin, and whenever I did, the crowds became bigger and bigger each time. One day Papa was there among them, watching, listening. He walked me home afterward, saying not a word until we were walking over the Accademia Bridge. 'So, Paolo,' he said, 'you prefer playing the violin to sweeping up in my barbershop, do you?'

"'Yes, Papa,' I replied. 'I'm afraid I do.'

"'Well then, I can see I shall just have to do my sweeping up myself.' He stopped then and put his hands on my shoulders. 'I shall tell you something, Paolo, and I want you never to forget it. When you play, I can listen to music again. You have made music joyful for me once more, and that is a wonderful gift you have given me. You go and be the great violinist you should be. I shall help you all I can. You will play heavenly music, and people will love you. Mama and I shall come to all your concerts, or as many as we can. But you have to promise me one thing: that until the day I die, you will never play Mozart in public, not in my hearing. It was Mozart we played so often in the camp. Never Mozart. Promise me.'

"So I promised. I have kept my promise to Papa all these years. He died two weeks ago, the last of the three of them to go. At my fiftieth birthday concert in London, I shall be playing Mozart, and I shall be playing it on Mama's violin, and I shall play it so well that he will love it, they will all love it, wherever they are."

I was still finishing my shorthand when I looked up and saw him coming toward me. He was offering me his violin.

"Here you are," he said. "Mama's violin. My violin. You can hold it if you like while we have some more mint tea. You'll have another cup, won't you? I make the best mint tea in Venice."

So I held Paolo Levi's violin for several precious minutes as we sat talking quietly over a last cup of tea. I asked him no more questions. There were none to ask. He talked of his love of Venice, and how wherever he was in the world he longed to be back home. It was the sounds he always missed: the church bells, the walking and talking, the chugging of boats, and the music in the streets. "Music belongs in the streets, where Benjamin played it," he said, "not in concert halls."

As I left, he looked me in the eye and said, still grasping my hand, "I am glad it was you I told."

"Why did you?" I asked. "Why did you tell me?"

"Because it was time to tell the truth. Because secrets are lies, and because you have eyes that are kind, like Benjamin's. But mostly because you didn't ask the Mozart question." +

from wombles to war

 There's a glowing time in early childhood of blessed and brief innocence. My children and my grandchildren lived it, and each time I have relived it with them. That's how I can be sure it happened to me, too. With each child and grandchild, it has been a chance to rediscover and indulge in that delightful and necessary conspiracy in which I suspend all the trials and tribulations of the real world I have come to know and share with them for a while the wondrous worlds of Trumpton, Thomas the Tank Engine, the Wombles, the Clangers, Winnie-the-Pooh, and Peter Rabbit. This is a time of pure delight, when we can live together for a while in contented reassuring worlds of stories, where we know for sure that all will be well for those we love, be it in Hundred Acre Wood or on Wimbledon Common. There may be an interfering Fat Controller or the threat of a Mr. McGregor, but we know it will all turn out just as we'd hoped it would, that Thomas and Peter and Pooh will be fine. It is a cuddly, comfortable time, and so it should be in those early years. There may be Wild Things or Gruffalos, a little scary perhaps, but never hiding-behind-the-sofa scary, more marvelous and magical than truly monstrous. Dark clouds in those early years should never be that dark, and should always give way to sunshine.

But then, gradually, there comes a time when he or she wants more from a story than mere comfort and reassurance. With a growing awareness of the difficulties and dangers and sadnesses of the world comes a need to find these complexities reflected in stories and poems. This gradual transition, this awakening of awareness, is not allowed to be as gradual as it once was. Indeed, it seems to be accelerating more rapidly with each generation.

For most children now, it is the screen that rules: the television, the video, the DVD, the PlayStation game, the computer. While there are, of course, many television programs and films sensitively and intelligently devised for children, many young children also tune in to programs and films enjoyed by their elders. And because one aspiration leads inevitably to another, very soon children are watching whatever it is that their older brothers and sisters watch or their parents watch, and much of this will be dealing with the world of adults. Just one episode of *EastEnders* or *The Bill* or *Hollyoaks* may involve domestic violence, crime, and death. A look at the six o'clock news might bring a natural disaster, murder, or war into the living room, all within the space of ten minutes.

So young children can be brought face-to-face with a hugely disturbing world, sometimes even before they can comprehend the difference between fact and fiction. The world of gentle dreams all too suddenly becomes a world of hideous nightmares. What took me twenty or more years to discover, to assimilate, to even begin to comprehend, now takes perhaps ten years for a child of today. Many efforts have been made over the years to slow this process down, because we know how traumatic it can be for a very young child to have to come to terms with the stark realities of some aspects of life in our modern world. But the truth is, whether we like it or not, it will be sooner rather than later that the children of the twenty-first century will have to learn to deal with issues and feelings hitherto thought to be the preserve of adults.

Despite its dangers, this fast-track growing does have some surprising benefits, one of them being that, in a sense, the worlds of the child and the adult have come closer together. More of our preoccupations seem to be commonly shared. Perhaps one of the great strengths of children's writing at present is that because the writer and reader no longer feel the experiences of childhood and adulthood to be as separate as they once were, writers feel they are free to tackle in their stories just about any subject that interests them, the presumption being that the child belongs to the same world, that the story will resonate with adult writer and child reader alike. So-called "crossover books" are no accident, I think. The blurring of this arbitrary division between child and adult seems one of the more positive outcomes of the accelerated growing of children. We have, it seems, been brought closer together.

I think I have always considered that we were close anyway, believing as I do that the child and the childishness in us is never "put away," as Saint Paul suggests it should be, but remains the heart of who we are, of what we grow up to be. So when I begin to think about writing a novel, I do not consider whether my story might be suitable for a child, nor even whether a child reader might like it. The only consideration is whether the story interests me sufficiently, whether I am, or can become, passionate about it. After all, I will be the writer and the first reader, and I am, I know, a grown-up child. I

simply hope my story will have the power to engage my readers whatever their age, that they will be as passionate about it
as I am by the time they have finished it. So I write as the story
dictates, not according to the age of any likely readership.

Like many of my fellow children's writers (and illustra-
tors and storytellers and poets, whose essential work in this
field goes so often unheralded), I have made hundreds of visits
to schools and conferences and festivals all over the world.
Questions are often challenging. From a nine-year-old last
year: "To be a writer you need knowledge and imagination.
Which is the more important of the two?" I am still thinking
about that. But more commonly asked is this: "In your books
like *War Horse*, like *Friend or Foe*, like *Billy the Kid*, like *Waiting
for Anya*, like *Private Peaceful*, you write about war. Why do
you do that? Why are they so sad?"

"Because," I reply, "I write about what I know, what I
care about. I know what war does to people, because I grew
up in London just after the Second World War, a London of
bomb sites and ration books. I played in bomb sites (surely
the best playgrounds ever made). We had cellars for dens,
crumbling walls to climb, and in among the rubble I made
endless discoveries. An old kettle, a shoe, a penny coin, a
burned book—they all became my treasures. Only later
came the growing awareness of what the war had done, not
just to buildings, but to people's lives.

"My mother often wept when she talked about the war.
On the mantelpiece was a photo of my uncle Pieter, who was
shot down in 1941, two years before I was born. He looked
back at me when I looked at him, and I knew he wanted to
say something but couldn't. I used to talk to him sometimes, I
remember. I wanted to get to know him.

"A friend of the family used to come to tea sometimes. My mother always told me I must not stare at him, but I always did. I could not stop myself. His face and hands were horribly scarred. I knew he had been shot down in the war and suffered dreadful burns. Here's what the war did. It burned flesh. It killed my uncle. It made my mother weep. So I grew up with the damage of war all around me. I learned that buildings you can put up again, but lives are wrecked forever. And why are the books sad, you asked? Because, believe me, war IS sad."

Flood, fire, famine, disease, a tsunami or an earthquake, terrorist bombings and war, devastation and disaster—television brings them all right into our homes. Punctuated by sports and advertisements and soaps, these catastrophes bombard our senses, each one an agony we are invited to share from the safety and comfort of our living rooms. But one horror is all too soon superseded by another on our screens, our attention and sympathy diverted. Old news, old disasters, and old wars are soon replaced in the public imagination and forgotten.

Vietnam, Cambodia, Rwanda, Bosnia, Kosovo, East Timor, Northern Ireland—remember them? The cruelties of war and ethnic cleansing seem as rife in modern times as they have ever been. We witness the horrors from afar, cocooned in our comfortable world. Of course we know it's not just on TV, but it might as well be. After all, it is not in our backyard, it is not for the most part our soldiers getting killed. We know it is vicious and violent and bloody, but it's over there! I once visited a village in France called Oradour, the scene of a massacre in the Second World War. The French have preserved the place just as the German occupiers left it, burned out, a village of the dead, a stark reminder to all of us of man's inhumanity to man. I need reminding. We all need reminding, I think, lest we grow hard, lest we forget. Let us never grow hard. Let us not forget.

I'm including here two stories of conflict, the first as seen by a child as it happened all around her in Bosnia, the second seen also by a child who was warned by his mother not to stare at the terrible scars of war on a man's face, but who did, often, and wrote about it more than fifty years later.

what does it feel like?

Seven o'clock, and it was just an ordinary kind of autumn morning, much like any other. The mist covered the valley floor, and the cows grazed along the river meadows. Sofia was still half asleep. The wild roses smelled of apples. Sofia pulled a fat rose hip from the hedgerow and idly split it open with her thumbnail. It was packed with seeds. A perfect spiderweb laced with mist linked the hedge to the gatepost. It trembled threateningly as she opened the gate into the meadow. She loved spiderwebs, but hated spiders.

Sofia sent the dog out to fetch in the cows and stayed leaning on the gate, her chin resting on her knuckles. Chewing nonchalantly, they meandered past her, ignoring her, all except Myrtle, who glanced with baleful eyes and licked deep into her nose. "Bad-tempered old cow," Sofia muttered. And she followed

Myrtle back along the lane toward the milking parlor. She could hear Mother singing inside, "Raining in My Heart." Buddy Holly again, always Buddy Holly.

Sofia wandered home, picking the last of the seeds out of the rose hip. She was deep in her thoughts. Mother did all the milking these days. She had since Father went off with the other men to the war. He had been gone nearly three months now, and still there had been no news. No news was good news. Mother said that often. Sofia believed her, but she knew that was only because she needed to believe her. It was hope rather than belief. There was a photo of Father on top of the piano at home. A team photo, after the village won the local soccer league last year. He was the one with the droopy mustache and balding head, crouching down in the front and holding his arms out in triumph.

There had been little warning of his going. He'd just come out with it at breakfast one morning. Nan had tried to talk him out of it, but he was adamant. Mother and Nan held hands and tried not to cry. "There are five of us going from the village," Father had said. "We've got to, don't you see? Else the war will come here, and we none of us want that, do we?"

The fighting was somewhere down south, a long way away,

Sofia knew that much. People had talked of little else now for a year or more. She'd seen pictures of it on the television. There was the little girl without any legs, lying on a hospital bed. She'd never forgotten that. She never wanted to be without her legs, never. And at school, Mr. Kovacs drew maps on the board, banged the desk, flashed his eyes, and said that we had to fight for what was ours if we wanted to keep it. All of us had to fight if need be, he said. But until the day Father left, none of it seemed at all real to Sofia. Even now, she had seen no tanks or planes. She had heard no guns. She had asked Nan about the war—Mother didn't like to talk about it—about why Father was fighting.

"Because they want our land. They always have," she'd said. "And because we hate them. We always have. We've hated them for hundreds of years."

"And do they hate us?" Sofia had asked.

"I suppose they must," Nan had said.

Sofia remembered the last day Father had been with them. She had come home from school and he'd been there all smiling and smelling of the wood he'd been sawing. That evening was the last time they'd been milking together. She smiled as she recalled how Myrtle had whipped her mucky tail across Father's face. "Bad-tempered old cow," he'd said, wiping his face with the back of his hand. Sofia had laughed at the brown smudge on his face, and Father had chased her out of the parlor. She thought then of his strong, calloused hands and loved them.

Nan was calling her from her thoughts. She hurried Sofia through her breakfast, grumbling all the time that the telephone was not working, that the electricity was cut off, too.

"I can't understand it," Nan said. "Maybe there's thunder close by, but it doesn't feel like thunder." She sent Sofia on her way to school, with a whiskery kiss.

It was ten to eight on Sofia's watch. Plenty of time. The farm was just on the edge of the village, not far. Sofia scuffled through the leaves, all the way down the road. By the time she reached the village square, there were no leaves left to scuffle. So she limped, one foot on the pavement, one in the road. She liked doing that. Sometimes, when no one was looking, she'd do the dance from *Singin' in the Rain.* This morning, though, she couldn't. There were too many people around, but very little traffic, she noticed, just a few bicycles. She crossed the road into the square. The café chairs were already out, and as usual, Mighty Martha was scrubbing the pavement on her hands and knees. She looked up and blew the hair out of her face. Mighty Martha was the only famous person ever to be born in the village. She had won an Olympic silver medal for throwing the discus more than twenty years before. Discus and medal hung proudly side by side on the café wall under a photo of Mighty Martha standing on a podium, smiling and waving. She was always smiling. That was why everyone wasn't just proud of her; they loved her, too. It helped that she also happened to make the best apple cake in the entire world. That was why her café was always full, even at this early hour. She was smiling at Sofia now.

"Better hurry," she called out. "Kovacs will have your guts for garters if you're late."

Sofia turned into School Lane. She could hear the bell going now. She'd just make it. But then she stopped. It wasn't only the bell she was hearing. There was a distant rumble that sounded like thunder. So Nan had been right. There was thunder. Sofia looked up at the mountains. It couldn't be thunder. There were no dark clouds. In fact, there were no clouds at all, just jagged white peaks sharp against a clear blue sky.

That was the moment Sofia remembered last night's geography homework: "Mountain Ranges of the World." She'd left it behind. She fought back the panic rising inside her and tried to think. Both the choices open to her were bad ones. She could run home to fetch it and be late for school, very late, or she could tell

Mr. Kovacs that she'd left it at home by mistake, but then he wouldn't believe her. Either way, Mr. Kovacs would "have her guts for garters." Sofia chose what seemed to be the least painful option. She would fetch her homework and, on the way there and back, concoct some credible excuse for being late. She ran back across the square with Mighty Martha shouting after her, "Where are you off to?" Sofia waved but did not reply.

The quickest way home was through the graveyard, but Sofia rarely took it. This morning she had to. She usually avoided the graveyard because Granddad had been buried there only two years before in the family grave, and Nan went up there twice a week with fresh flowers. To pass the grave and see the flowers only made Sofia sad about Granddad all over again. There was a photograph of him on the grave that looked at her as she passed. She hated looking at it. She still half expected him to talk to her, which was silly and she knew it. Nonetheless she always hurried past him before he had a chance to speak.

As she ran, her foot turned on a loose stone. She heard her ankle crack. It gave under her, and she fell heavily, grazing her knees and hands. She sat up to nurse her ankle, which was throbbing now with such pain that she thought she might faint.

When she finally looked up, Granddad was gazing at her sternly from his photograph. She tried to hold back her tears. He'd always hated for her to cry. She rocked back and forth, groaning, watching the blood from her knee trickle down her leg.

Her books were scattered all over the path, her English book facedown in a puddle. She was reaching for it when she heard the thunder again, much closer this time. For just a moment she thought it might be guns, but then she dismissed that at once. The war was down south, miles away; everyone said so. Mr. Kovacs's maps said so. By now she was hearing an incongruous rattling and squeaking, more like the noise of a dozen tractors trailing the plows on the road. She stood up on her one good foot and looked down into the village.

Two tanks rumbled into the square from different ends of the village, engines roaring and smoking. Behind them came six open trucks. When they reached the square, they all stopped. Soldiers jumped out. The engines died. The smoke lifted through the trees and a silence fell over the village. Doors opened; heads appeared at windows.

Mighty Martha stood alone in the square, her scrubbing brush in her hand. The soldiers were gazing around like tourists as the last of them climbed down out of the trucks. Mighty Martha's dog barked at them from the door of the café, his hackles raised. All the soldiers wore headbands, red headbands, except one, who was wearing a beret, and there was a gun belt around his waist, like a cowboy. The soldiers—Sofia thought there must be perhaps thirty in all gathered around him—then wandered off in small groups into the narrow streets as if they were going to explore. They had their rifles slung over their shoulders. Sofia wondered if Father wore a red band around his head like they did. The man in the black beret leaned back against a tank, crossed his legs, and lit up a cigarette. Mighty Martha stood watching him for a few moments. Then she dropped her scrubbing brush into the bucket, slapped her hands dry, and strode into the café.

Sofia gathered up her books and hobbled down the path back toward the square. Mighty Martha would see to her ankle for her, as she had done once before when Sofia had fallen off her bike. Martha had been a nurse once. She knew about these things, and besides, Sofia wanted to know what was going on. She wanted to get a closer look at the tanks. The homework and Mr. Kovacs had been forgotten.

She had got as far as the public bathroom on the corner of the square when she saw Martha coming out of the café. She was holding a rifle. Suddenly she stopped, brought it to her shoulder, and pointed it at the cowboy soldier.

"This is our village," she cried, "and you will never take it from us, never."

A shot rang out and the rifle fell from Martha's hands. Her head twisted unnaturally on her neck and nodded loose for a moment like a puppet's head. Then she just collapsed, fell face forward on the cobbles, and was still. The cowboy soldier was walking toward her, his pistol in his hand. He turned Martha over with the toe of his boot.

Sofia darted into the bathroom, ran to the ladies' room, closed the door behind her, and bolted it. She sat down, squeezed her eyes shut tight, and tried not to believe what she had just witnessed. She heard herself moaning and stopped breathing so that the moaning, too, would stop. But it did not. She knew then that it came from outside.

She climbed up on the toilet seat. The frosted window was open a centimeter or two. They were coming into the square from every corner. Mr. Kovacs and all the schoolchildren came in twos down School Lane, the soldiers hustling them along. The children seemed more bewildered than frightened, except little Ilic, who clutched Mr. Kovacs's hand and cried openly. None of them had seen Martha yet. The cowboy soldier was climbing up onto a tank. He stood legs apart, thumbs hooked into his belt, and watched as everyone was marshaled into the square.

The doctor was there, pushing old Mrs. Marxova in her wheelchair. Swathed in a shawl, her face ashen, she was pointing down at Martha. Some people were still in their dressing gowns and slippers. Stefan and Peter from the garage had their hands high in the air, a soldier behind them, jabbing them in their backs with his rifle barrel. Up the road from the bridge, Sofia could see all the old folks from the retirement home, a couple of soldiers herding them along like cattle. They would pass by right underneath the bathroom window. It was they who were moaning and wailing. Sofia drew back so she wouldn't be seen. She waited until they had gone and then peered out again.

The square was filling. The schoolchildren were gathered around Mr. Kovacs, who was talking to them, trying to reassure them, but the children had seen Martha. Everyone had seen Martha. Mrs. Marxova held her hands over her eyes and was shaking her head. The doctor was leaning over Martha and feeling her neck, then he was listening to her chest. After a while he took his jacket off and covered her face.

She waited until they had gone and then peered out again.

Little Ilic saw his mother and ran screaming across the square. One by one now the children ignored all Mr. Kovacs's attempts to keep them together and went off to search for their mothers. Once found, the children clung to their mothers passionately as if they would never let go.

That was when Sofia saw Mother and Nan, arms linked, being marched into the square. All Sofia's neighbors were with them, too. They'd even found Mr. Dodovic, who lived alone in his hut and kept his bees high up in the mountainside. Like all the men, he, too, had his hands in the air. Mother went straight over to Mr. Kovacs and took him by the arm. Mr. Kovacs shook his head at her. Sofia longed to cry out, to run to her. But something inside her held her back. Everyone in the village was corraled in the square by now and surrounded by the soldiers.

A machine gun was being set up on the steps of the post office and another by the garage on the corner. Mother was talking to the doctor and looking about her frantically. Nan had sat down in a chair outside the café and was staring blankly at Martha.

The cowboy soldier on the tank held up his hands. The hush was almost instantaneous. Even the children stopped crying, except for Mrs. Dungonic's new baby. Mrs. Dungonic picked her up and shushed her over her shoulder. The whole square was silent now, expectant.

"You have seen now what happens if you resist," the cowboy soldier began. "No one will come to help you. All the telephone lines are cut. All the roads are blocked. You will do what we say. We do not want to harm any more of you, but if you make us, we will. Have no doubt about it. We are simply moving you. This land does not belong to you. You have been squatting here on our land for over three hundred years. You took it from my people. You stole it from us. Now we are taking back what is rightfully ours." No one said a word. "But we do not want to live in your stinking hovels, so we are going to burn the whole place down. By this evening it will be as if it never existed. That way you'll have nothing to come back to, will you?" Still no one said anything.

Sofia was screaming inside herself, *Don't just stand there. Tell him he can't do it. Stop him. What's the matter with you all?*

"Now," the cowboy soldier went on as he swaggered along the side of his tank, "here's what you do. The men, if you can call yourselves men, you get in those trucks outside the shop. Be good boys now. Off you go." No one moved. He took out his pistol and pointed it at the doctor. "Go," he said quietly.

"Where are we going?" the doctor asked.

"You'll see," replied the cowboy soldier.

Sofia ducked. A soldier was walking toward the bathroom. Sofia prayed, her eyes shut tight, fists and jaws clenched. *Don't let him come in. Don't let him come in. Be good, God. Don't let him come in.*

He came in. She heard the tap running into the basin. He was drinking. Then he spoke. "Forgive me," he whispered. "Dear God, forgive me. I begged the captain. I begged him, but he wouldn't listen. Rats, he said, they breed like rats. You burn rats out. You destroy them. But they're not rats; they're flesh and blood. Oh, God, oh, God." He was sobbing and then he was kicking the wall. That was the moment Sofia shifted her weight onto her bad ankle and slipped. The sobbing stopped at once. Sofia shrank back as the footsteps came toward her. She could hear his breathing through the door.

"Whoever you are"—his voice was urgent but gentle— "whoever's in there, just listen to me. Whatever happens, stay where you are. Believe me, where they're going, you don't want to go. Stay put. Don't move. I'll do what I can." And then he was gone.

It was some time after he'd left before Sofia screwed up enough courage to look out her window again. When she did,

singing for mrs. pettigrew

she saw the last of the men from the village climbing up into the truck. There were two truckloads of them. A fierce anger welled up inside her. They were going like lambs, all of them. What of the rousing, triumphal songs they had sung so often in the café? What of Mr. Kovacs's defiant exhortations that everyone must defend the homeland? How could they leave the women and the children without even a word of protest? How could they? The men were just sitting there with bowed heads, Mr. Kovacs weeping openly. She hated him then even more than the cowboy soldier. She hated them all.

"Good," said the cowboy soldier smiling. "Good boys. Now, women and children to the other trucks, and don't worry yourselves; you'll all meet up again soon enough. Hurry now." He waved his pistol, and the women and children drifted slowly, reluctantly, across to the other side of the square. The soldiers stood by and looked on as they struggled to clamber in. Only one of them stepped forward to pick up the smaller children and hand them up. Sofia wondered if it was her soldier. She hoped it was. He had long hair to his shoulders and a mustache like Father's. He seemed very young to be a soldier.

It took three of them to lift Mrs. Marxova out of her wheelchair and up into the truck. They were not gentle with her. One of them kicked away her chair so that it rolled down the road, hitting a curb and turning over in the gutter. They laughed at that. Mother helped Nan up into the truck beside her and they sat down together, Nan's head resting on her shoulder. The trucks started up. Mother was calling for her now, crying.

Sofia made up her mind in that instant. She had to be with them. Why should she trust the soldier? She didn't even know him. She had hardly seen him. She unlocked the door and ran past the basins, forgetting her ankle. She slipped and fell by the doorway. By the time she was up on her feet again, she could hear the trucks already moving off. It was too late. Maybe, she thought, maybe the soldier was right after all. Maybe she was safer here, undiscovered. She hobbled back into the bathroom and shut the door. She climbed up just in time to see the last truck leaving the square and her mother's scarved head still turning, still looking. She was crying.

The cowboy soldier leaped down off his tank. "You know what to do. I don't want a building left standing. Understand? Nothing. You'll find all the gas you need in the garage. Use hay, sticks, anything that'll burn. If it won't burn, then blow it up." The soldiers cheered at that. Whooping and yelling, they scat-tered in all directions, some diving directly into the houses on the

singing for mrs. pettigrew

square and others running off down the village streets. Soon the square was left to the cowboy soldier, who sat down on a bench and lit up another cigarette. He blew smoke rings into the air and poked his finger through them. Martha's dog was snuffling around her body, his tail between his legs.

Sofia could not look anymore. She sat down. The blood had congealed on her leg. She took off her sock. Her ankle was puffed up and gray.

A window shattered somewhere in the village, then another, then another. Distantly, a gun began to chatter and did not stop.

"Are you still in there?" It was the soldier's voice from below her window.

"Yes," she replied at once, without thinking.

"For God's sake, don't try to run. You'll be seen. They'll kill you if they see you. They mustn't leave any witnesses."

"My mother, my nan. They were in the truck. Where have you taken them? Where have they gone?"

"You don't want to know," said the soldier. "Just worry about yourself. And don't look out the window. They'll see you. I could see the shape of your head from across the square. Keep down. I can't stay." Sofia heard him walk away. She wanted to ask him so much more but could not risk calling out. She sat down on the toilet and tried to gather her thoughts, but nothing would come but tears. Racked with sobbing, Sofia put her head between her knees and hugged herself into a tight ball and closed her eyes. So she sat for hour after hour as they burned the village around her. Trying not to listen, not to smell.

The first explosion was from far away, but all the same, it rocked the building, blasted her ears, and left a ringing inside her head that would not stop. The next was closer, in the square itself, maybe the post office, she thought, and the next shortly afterward was even closer still. Perhaps the café. She bit her lip till it bled, determined not to scream, not to give herself away. When plaster crashed down from the ceiling onto her shoulders, she could stand it no longer. She lifted her head and screamed and screamed. Through her own screaming, through the whistle in her ears, she heard the whoosh and crackle of the flames outside, the roar of the roofs collapsing, and always the soldiers whooping.

Then she saw smoke drifting in under her door, thick smoke that would stifle the life out of her. She had to get away. She climbed up onto the seat and put her nose to the window to breathe in the last of the cleaner air. That was when the tanks began to fire from under the trees, pounding, pounding, pounding. She fell backward onto the floor, back down into the smoke. She rolled into a corner, covering her face, her mouth, her ears, clenching herself into herself as tight as she would fit. Then she prayed. The picture she had seen on television of the child without any legs flashed into her head. "Please, God, I want my legs. I need my legs. Let me die if you want, but I want my legs. I want my legs."

The smoke was thinning. Suddenly she could breathe without coughing, then there were voices outside.

"The bathrooms. Don't forget the bathrooms." It was the cowboy soldier. "A grenade will do it."

"Hardly worth the trouble, Captain," said another. Her soldier, her soldier's voice. "It's not as if there's anyone left to piss in it, is there? And anyway, why don't we leave it there as a monument. All that's left of them, their bathrooms."

The cowboy soldier laughed. "Good. Very good. I like it. Some bonfire, eh?" They were walking away now. The cowboy soldier went on, "D'you see the mosque come down? Obstinate beggar. Took twenty rounds to topple him. This heat gives a man a thirst, eh? Let's get beer."

"Why not?" said Sofia's soldier.

There were no more shootings after that, no more explosions, but Sofia stayed where she was, curled up on the floor of the bathroom. She could hear the soldiers carousing in the square and the sound of smashing beer bottles. One crashed against the window above her head, shattering the glass. Shortly after, their laughter was drowned out by the noise of the tank engines start‑ ing up. They were calling each other. They were going. She waited a few minutes more until she was sure the tanks were on the move, their engines revving. Then she climbed up and looked out. The two tanks were rumbling away out of sight, belching black smoke out behind them. They were gone.

Everywhere she looked was utter destruction. The village was a flaming, smoking ruin. Like all the other buildings, the café had no roof. Flames licked out of the windows, leaping across the road into the trees. The parked cars were blackened shells now, the tires still burning furiously. The front of the shop had entirely caved in. Sofia got down, opened the door, and hobbled out into the square. The minaret had fallen right across School Lane, obliterating the houses beneath. Martha still lay outside her café, but now her dog was beside her. He was not moving. Sofia sat down on the bench in the middle of the square, where she was farthest from the heat of the fires. She had no tears left to cry.

She was still sitting there late that evening when the reporters came in their Land Rover. She was rocking back and forth and there was a cow beside her, grazing the grass. She was humming "Raining in My Heart." She looked up at them as they approached.

"Hello," she said. "That's Myrtle. She's come to find me. She needs milking."

"Is this your village?" asked a reporter, pushing a microphone at her. Sofia looked at him blankly. "What does it feel like to see it like this?" he went on. "And what do you think of the people who've done it? Where the hell is everyone, anyway?"

"I've got my legs," said Sofia, and she smiled. "I've got my legs. God is great." ✛

half a man

When I was very little, more than half a century ago now, I used to have nightmares. You don't forget nightmares. The nightmare was always the same. It began with a face, a twisted, tortured face that screamed silently, a face without hair or eyebrows, a skull more than a face, a skull which was covered in puckered, scarred skin stretched over the cheekbones. It was Grandpa's face and he was staring at me out of his scream. And always the face was on fire, flames licking out of his ears and mouth.

I remember I always tried to force myself to wake up, so that I wouldn't have to endure the rest of it. But I knew every time that the rest would follow, however hard I tried to escape—that my nightmare would not release me, would not allow me to wake until the whole horrible tale had played itself out.

I saw a great ship ablaze on the ocean. There were men on fire jumping overboard as she went down, then swimming in a sea where the water burned and boiled around them. I saw Grandpa swimming toward a lifeboat, but it was packed with sailors and there was no room for Grandpa. He begged them to let him on, but they wouldn't. Behind him, the ship's bow lifted out of the sea, and the whole ship groaned like a wounded beast in her death throes. Then she went down, slipping slowly under the waves, gasping great gouts of steam in the last of her agony. A silence came over the burning sea. Grandpa was clinging to the lifeboat now, his elbows hooked over the side. That was when I realized that I was in the lifeboat with the other sailors. He saw me looking down at him and reached out his hand for help. It was a hand with no fingers.

I would wake up then, shaking in my terror and knowing even now that my nightmare was not over. For my nightmare would always seem to happen just a day or two before Grandpa came to stay. It was a visit I always dreaded. He didn't come to see us in London very often, every couple of years at most, and usually at Christmas. Thinking about it now, I suppose this was part of the problem. There were perfectly good reasons why we didn't and couldn't see more of him. He lived far away, on the Isles of Scilly, so it was a long way for him to come, and expensive, too.

Besides which, he hated big cities like London. I'm sure if I'd seen him more often, I'd have gotten used to him—used to his face and his hands and his silent, uncommunicative ways.

I don't blame my mother and father. I can see now why they were so tense before each visit. Being as taciturn and unsmiling as he was, Grandpa can't have been an easy guest. But, even so, they did make it a lot worse for me than they needed to. Just before Grandpa came there were always endless warnings, from Mother in particular (he was my grandpa on my mother's side), about how I mustn't upset him, how I mustn't leave my toys lying about on the living room floor because he didn't see very well and might trip over them, how I mustn't have the television on too much because Grandpa didn't like noise. But most of all they drummed into me again and again that whatever I did, I must not under any circumstances stare at him—that it was rude, that he hated people staring at him, particularly children.

I tried not to; I tried very hard. When he first arrived, I would always try to force myself to look at something else. Once I remember it was a Christmas decoration, a red paper bell hanging just above his head in the front hall. Sometimes I would make myself look very deliberately at his waistcoat perhaps, or the gold watch chain he always wore. I'd fix my gaze on anything just as long as it was nowhere near the forbidden places, because I knew that once I started looking at his forbidden face or his forbidden hands, I wouldn't be able to stop myself.

But every time, sooner or later, I'd do it; I'd sneak a sly look. And very soon that look became a stare. I was never at all revolted by what I saw. If I had been, I could have looked away easily. I think I was more fascinated than anything else, and horrified, too, because I'd been told something of what had happened to him in the war. I saw the suffering he had gone through in his deep blue eyes—eyes that hardly ever blinked, I noticed. Then I'd feel my mother's eyes boring into me, willing me to stop staring, or my father would kick me under the table. So I'd look at Grandpa's waistcoat—but I could only manage it for a while. I couldn't help myself. I had to look again at the forbidden places. He had three half-fingers on one hand and no fingers at all on the other. His top lip had almost completely disappeared, and one of his ears was little more than a hole in his head.

As I grew up, I'd often ask about how exactly it had happened. My mother and father never seemed to want to tell me much about it. They claimed they didn't know any more than they'd told me already—that Grandpa had been in the merchant navy in the Second World War, that his ship had been torpedoed in the Atlantic, and he'd been terribly burned. He'd been adrift in a boat for days and days, they told me, before he'd been picked up. He'd spent the rest of the war in a special hospital.

Every time I looked at his face and hands, the story seemed to want to tell itself again in my head. I so much wanted to know more. And I wanted to know more about my grandmother, too, but that was a story that made everyone even more tight-lipped. I knew she was named Annie, but I had never met her and no one ever talked about her. All anyone would ever say was that she had "gone away" a very long time ago, before I was born. I longed to ask Grandpa himself about his ship being torpedoed, about my grandmother, too, but I never dared, not even when I was older and got to know him a lot better.

I must have been about twelve when I first went to see him on my own in the Scilly Isles for my summer break, and by then the nightmares had gone. That's not to say I wasn't still apprehensive in those first few days after I arrived. But I was always happy to be there, happy just to get out of London. I'd go and stay with him in his cottage on Bryher—a tiny island; only about eighty people lived there. He had no electricity, only a generator in a shed out-side, which he'd switch off before he went to bed. The cottage wasn't much more than a shed, either. It was a different world for me and I loved it. He lived by himself and lived simply. The place smelled of warm damp and paraffin oil and fish—we had fish for almost every meal. He made some kind of living out of catching lobsters and crabs. How he managed to go fishing with his hands as they were, I'll never know. But he did.

It was years before I discovered why he never smiled. It was because he couldn't. It was too painful. The skin simply wouldn't stretch. When he laughed, which wasn't often, it was always with a straight face. And when he smiled, it was with his eyes only. I'd never understood that when I was little. His eyes were the same blue as the sea around Scilly on a fine day. He was silent, I discovered, because he liked to keep himself to himself. I'm a bit the same, so I didn't mind. He wasn't at all unkind or morose, just quiet. He'd read a lot in the evenings, for hours, anything about boats—Arthur Ransome, C. S. Forester, and Patrick O'Brian. He didn't have a television, so I'd read them, too. I think I must have read every book Arthur Ransome wrote during my time on Scilly.

During the day he'd let me do what I liked. I could run free. I'd wander the island all day; I'd go climbing on the rocks on

Samson Hill or Droppy Nose Point. I'd go swimming in Rushy Bay, shrimping off Green Bay. But as I got older, he'd ask me to go out fishing with him more and more. He liked the company, I think, or maybe it was because he needed the help, even if he never said so. I'd catch wrasse and pollack for baiting his lobster pots. I'd help him haul them in and extract the catch. We would work almost silently together, our eyes meeting from time to time. Sometimes he'd catch me staring at him as he had when I was little. All those years later and I still couldn't help myself. But now it was different. Now all the fear had gone. Now I knew him well enough to smile at him when our eyes met, and, as I was later to find out, he understood perfectly well why I was staring at him, at his forbidden face, his forbidden hands.

It wasn't until the summer I left school that Grandpa first told me himself about what had happened to him when his ship went down. He talked more these days, but never as much as the day we saw the gannets. We were out in his fishing boat. We'd picked up the pots, caught a few mackerel for supper, and were coming back in a lumpy sea around the back of Bryher, when a pair of gannets flew over and dived together, spearing the sea just ahead of us. "See that, Grandpa?" I cried. "Aren't they brilliant?"

"Better than brilliant," he said. "They bring you good luck, you know."

We watched the gannets surface, swallow their catch, and take off again. We caught each other's eye and smiled, enjoying the moment together.

"You know what I like about you, Michael?" he went on. "You look at me. Most people don't. Your mother doesn't, and she's my own daughter. She looks away. Most people look away. Not that I blame them. I did once. Not anymore. But you don't look away." He smiled. "You've been having sneaky old looks at me ever since you were knee-high to a grasshopper. If you looked away, it was only to be polite—I always knew that. You've always wanted to ask me, haven't you? You wanted to know, didn't you? How this happened, I mean."

He touched his face. "I never told anyone before, not your mother, not even Annie. I just told them what they needed to know and no more, that my ship went down and after a few days in a lifeboat I got picked up. That's all I said. The rest they could see for themselves." He was looking straight ahead of him, steering the boat as he was talking.

"I was a handsome-enough devil before that—looked a bit like you do now. Annie and me got married a couple of years

We caught each other's eye and smiled, enjoying the moment together.

before the war broke out. A year later, I was in the merchant navy, in a convoy coming back from America. My third trip, it was." He looked out toward Scilly Rock and wiped his face with the back of his hand. "It was a day like this, the day we copped it—the day I became half a man. Early evening, it happened. I'd seen ships go down before, dozens of them, and every time I thanked God it wasn't me. Now it was my turn.

"I was on watch when the first torpedo struck. Never saw it coming. The first hit us amidships. The second blew off the stern—took it right off. All hell broke loose. A great ball of fire came roaring through the ship, set me on fire, and cooked me like a sausage. Jim—Jim Channing—he came from Scilly, too— him and me were mates, always were, even at school, joined up together—he smothered the flames, put them out. Then he helped me to the side. I'd never even have got that far without Jim. He made me jump. I didn't want to, because the sea was on fire. But he made me. He had hold of me and swam me away from the ship, so we wouldn't get sucked down, he said. He got me to a lifeboat. There were too many in it already and they didn't want us."

I could see it! I could see it in my head. It was straight out of my nightmare.

"Jim said that he could hang on to the side, but I'd been burnt and they had to help me into the boat. In the end they did, and Jim clung on beside me, still in the water, and we talked. We had to talk, and keep talking, Jim told me, so we didn't go to sleep, because if we went to sleep, like as not we'd never wake up again. So we told each other all the stories we knew: *Peter Rabbit,* the *Just So Stories* — anything we could remember. When we ran out of stories, we tried singing songs instead: 'Ten Green Bottles,' 'Oranges and Lemons,' anything. Time and again I dropped off to sleep, but Jim would always wake me up. Then one time I woke and Jim just wasn't there. He was gone. I've thought about Jim every day of my life since, but I've never spoken about him, until now.

"He's out there, Michael. Jim's out there, down in the deep somewhere. They all are, all the lads that went down in that ship, good lads. And there's been plenty of times since, I can tell you, when I wished to God I'd gone down with them."

He said nothing more for a while. I'd never heard him talk like this before, never. But he hadn't finished yet.

"All we saw for days on end were gannets," he went on. "Except once we did see a whale, a ruddy great whale. But that was all. No ships. No airplanes. Nothing. Just sea and sky. Some of the lads were burnt even worse than I was. They didn't last long. We were out there on the open ocean for a week or more. No food, no water. I lost count of the days and the nights. By then I didn't know anymore who was alive and who was dead, and what's more I didn't care. I only knew I was still alive. That was all that mattered to me. I lived on nothing but hope, and a dream. I had a dream and I clung on to it. I dreamt of getting back to Annie, of coming home. I thought if I dreamt it hard enough, hoped for it hard enough, it must come true.

"Then, one morning, I wake up and there's this huge destroyer right there alongside us and men looking down over the side and waving and shouting. I thought I was still in my dream, but I wasn't. Only three of us out of that whole lifeboat survived. They patched me up as best they could and shipped me home. The next thing I knew, I was in this hospital, down in Sussex it was, East Grinstead. That's where they put the pieces of me together again, like a sort of jigsaw puzzle, but the pieces were skin and bone and flesh. The trouble was, there were some pieces of my jigsaw missing, so they had a bit of a job, which is why I still look a bit of a mess. But I wasn't the worst in that hospital, not by a long shot.

"Dr. McIndoe, he was called. Wonderful man he was, a

genius. It was him that did it, put us back together, and I'm not just talking about the operations. He was a magician in the oper-ating theater, all right. But it's what he did afterwards for us. He made us feel right again inside, like we mattered, like we weren't monster men. It was a hospital full of men like me, but mostly air-force boys. We were all together, every one of us patched up in one way or another, so it didn't matter what we looked like even when we went out and about. Everyone treated us right: nurses and doctors, everyone. Annie came to see me when she could. Right away I saw she didn't look at me the same, didn't speak to me like I was normal, like the nurses did. She still loved me, I think, but all she saw was a monster man.

"After a while, when the war was over, I left the hospital and came home to Annie, home to Scilly. My dream had come true, I thought. But of course it hadn't. I soon found that out. Annie tried—tried her best. I tried, too. We had a baby—your mother, Michael—but Annie still wasn't looking at me. I drank too much, said things I shouldn't have said. She did, too: told me I should stop feeling sorry for myself, that I wasn't the man she'd married anymore. Then we just stopped talking to one another. One day I came back home from a day's fishing and she'd left, just like that, taking my little girl, your mother, with her. She'd had enough. I don't blame her, not anymore. No one wants a monster for a husband. No one wants half a man, and that's what I was, Michael, half a man. That's what I still am. But I blamed her then. I hated her. Every day it's all I could think of, how much I hated her.

"I lived with that hate inside me most of my life. Hate, anger, call it what you will. It's like a cancer. It eats away at you. She wouldn't let me see my little girl, even when she was older. I never forgave her for that. She said I drank too much, which was true—said I'd frighten the girl too much. Maybe she was right. Maybe she was right."

It wasn't the moment to say anything, so I didn't. We fell into our silence again.

We unloaded the catch, moored the boat, and walked together back home up the hill. We cooked the mackerel and sat eating it, still in silence. I was silent because I was reliving his story in my head. But I had one thing I needed to say.

"She wasn't right," I told him. "Annie should have let you see your own daughter. Everyone has a right to see their own child."

"Maybe," he replied. "But the truth is, I think I do frighten your mother a little, even now. So Annie was right, in her way. Your mother came to see me for the first time after she'd left school, when she wasn't a little girl anymore; practically grown up, she was. She came without ever asking her mother, to find out who her father was, she said, because she hadn't ever known me, not properly. She was kind to me. She's always been kind to me ever since. But even now she can't look me in the eye like you do. She writes letters, keeps in touch, calls me Dad, lets me visit, does her best by me, always has. And I'm grateful, don't get me wrong. But every time I came to you for Christmas when you were little, I longed for her just to look at me. She wants to, but she can't. And she's angry, too, like I was. She can't forgive her mother for what she did either, for taking her away from her dad. She hasn't spoken to her mother now in over twenty years. Time's come to forgive and forget; that's what I think."

So now I knew the whole story for the first time. We relapsed after that into our usual, quiet ways for the rest of the summer. But by the time I left, I think I was closer to him than I have ever been to anyone else in my life.

I went back a year later, this time with my mother to visit him in the hospital. He was already too ill to get out of bed. He said he was a lucky man because he could see the sea from his bed. He died the second night we were there. He'd left a letter for me on the mantelpiece in his cottage.

Dear Michael,

See that they bury me at sea. I want to be with Jim and the others. I want Annie there, and I want your mother there too. I want you all there together. I want things put right. Thanks for looking at me like you did.

Love,

Grandpa

A few days later, Annie came over to Scilly for the funeral. She held hands with my mother as Grandpa's ashes were scattered out beyond Scilly Rock. We were lucky. We had a fine day for it. The gannets were flying, and everyone was together, just as Grandpa had wanted. So he was right about gannets. Grandpa was right about a lot of things. But he wasn't half a man. ✚

i was there with horses, too

I was in my local pub, the Duke of York, in Iddesleigh in deepest Devon. It was twenty-five years ago now. "Are you writing another book, Michael?" said the old man sitting opposite me by the fire, cradling his pint. I told him I had come across an old painting of a cavalry charge in the First World War. The British cavalry was charging up a hill toward the German position, one or two horses already caught up in the barbed wire. I was trying, I told him, to write a story of the First World War as seen through the eyes of a horse. "I was there in 1916," the old man told me, his eyes filling with tears. "I was there with horses, too." He talked on for hours about the horse he'd loved and left behind at the end of the war, how the old horse had been sold off to the French butchers for meat. Afterward I went back home, sat down, and wrote my first novel about the First World War, *War Horse.*

Having written several other novels and short stories about war, some five years ago I was invited to Ypres ("Wipers" to the British Tommy of the First World War) to an international conference of writers who had written on this difficult subject. On visiting the In Flanders Fields Museum in Ypres, the most moving museum I have ever been in—you can hardly speak when you come out—I came across a telegram sent to a mother in England in 1916, informing her that her son had been shot for cowardice. I stood there, over-whelmed with sadness, feeling something of the great grief which that mother must have felt on receiving this terrible news, knowing her life and her family's lives must have been blighted forever.

I had the good fortune then to meet the museum's curator, Piet Chielens, and I asked him if he knew how many British soldiers had been executed in the First World War. Over three hundred, he said—some for desertion, some for cowardice, and two for falling asleep at their posts. I read some of the records of their trials, many of which lasted less than half an hour. Half an hour for a man's life. In all of this I noted a presumption of guilt, not innocence. Often soldiers were unrepresented; often no witnesses were called in their defense. Many were clearly shell-shocked—a trauma already recog-nized and understood at the time. Many men, officers mostly, suffering from shell shock were sent home for treatment. Not so these unfortunates. Condemned as "worthless men," three thousand were sentenced to death. Of these, over three hun-dred were shot.

One case I read concerned a young soldier who had fought all through the Battle of the Somme in 1916, witnessed the slaughter and the horror, but one day decided in rest camp that he couldn't stand the sound of the guns any longer. He walked out, was arrested, court-martialed, and condemned to death. Six weeks later he was taken out at dawn and shot. Men from his own company were forced to make up the firing squad. To protest and to honor the man they had been forced to kill, they stood by his grave all day till sunset.

That there was little justice for these men I have no doubt. That these were political, military tribunals, seeking at the outset to condemn, *"pour encourager les autres,"* I have no doubt. Knowing this, seeing in my mind's eye that young man tied to a post one gray dawn in a field near Ypres in 1916, and knowing that successive governments in this country have refused both to acknowledge the injustices these men suffered and to pardon them—either would do—I decided to write, needed to write, the story of this young soldier. I called it *Private Peaceful,* the name of a dead soldier I'd found quite by chance on a grave in Bedford Cemetery, a Commonwealth War Graves cemetery just outside Ypres.

But this next story is about another war, about a private soldier from another country, Argentina, an enemy country at the time the story takes place. I saw him in a photograph. He was lying crumpled among rocks on top of a mountain in the Falklands. He may have been an enemy, but he was someone's son, someone's brother, someone's father, too, perhaps.

for carlos, a letter from your father

I have never forgotten my tenth birthday. All my other childhood birthdays are lost somewhere in the mists of memory, blurred by sameness, perhaps: the excitement of anticipation, the brief rapture of opening presents, and then the inevitable disappointment because birthdays, like Christmases, were always so quickly over. Not so my tenth.

It is not only because of the gleaming silver bike my mother gave me that I remember it so well. I tried it out at once, in my pajamas. In an ecstasy of joy and pride I rode it around and around the block, hoping all my friends would be up early and watching out their windows, admiring, and seething with envy, too. But even my memory of that has diminished over the years. It was when I came home, puffed out and glowing, and sat down for breakfast, that my mother gave me something else, too. It is this second gift that I have never forgotten. I can't honestly remember what happened to my beautiful bike. Either it rusted away at the back of the garage when I outgrew it or it was thrown away. I don't know. I do know that I still have this second gift, that I have never grown out of it and I will never throw it away.

She put down beside me on the kitchen table what looked at first like an ordinary birthday card. She didn't say who it was from, but I could see that there was something about this card that troubled her deeply.

"Who's it from?" I asked her. I wasn't that interested at first—after all, birthday cards were never as intriguing as presents. She didn't answer me. I picked up the envelope. There, written in handwriting I did not know, was my answer: For Carlos, a letter from your father.

The envelope had clearly been folded. It was dirty and there was a tear in one corner. The word father *was smeared and only just legible. I looked up and saw my mother's eyes filled with tears. I knew instantly she wanted me to ask no more questions. She simply said, "He wanted me to keep it for you, until your tenth birthday."*

So I opened the card and read.

Dearest Carlos,

I want to wish you first of all a very happy tenth birthday. How I would love to be with you on this special day. Maybe we could have gone riding together as I once did with my father on my birthday. Was it my tenth? I can't remember. I do remember we rode all day and picnicked on a high hill where the wind breathed through the long grass. I thought I could see forever from that hill. Or maybe we could have gone to a soccer match and howled together at the referee and leaped up and down when we scored.

But then maybe you don't like horses or soccer. Why should you have grown up like me? You are a different person, but with a little of me inside you, that's all. I do know that your mother and I would have sung "Happy Birthday" to you and watched your eyes light up when you opened your presents and as you blew out the candles on your cake.

But all I have to give, all I can offer, is this letter, a letter I hope you will never have to read, for if you are reading it now, it means that I am not with you and have never been with you, that I died ten years ago in some stupid, stupid war that killed me and many, many others, and like all wars did no one any good.

Dying, Carlos, as you know, comes to each of us. Strangely, I am not afraid, not as much as I have been. I think maybe that love has conquered my fear. I am filled with so much love for you, and such a sadness, too, a sadness I pray you will never have to know. It is the thought of losing you before I even get to know you that saddens me so. If I die in this terrible place, then we shall never meet, not properly, father to son. We shall never talk.

For a father to be parted from his son is always a terrible thing, yet if it has to be, then in a way I would rather it was now, this way, this soon. To have known you, to have watched you grow and then to have lost you, would surely be even worse. Or am I just telling myself that?

You will know me a little, I suppose, perhaps from photographs. And your mother may well have told you something about me, of my childhood, how I grew up on the farm in Patagonia and was riding horses almost before I could walk. Maybe she told you of our first meeting, when her car had a flat tire and I was riding by and stopped to change it for her. I am quite good at tinkering with motors—you have to be, on a farm. But I took a lot longer to change that tire than I needed to—if you know what I mean. By the time I had finished, I knew I loved her and wanted to spend my whole life with her. Later I learned that she went home afterward and told her sister that she'd met this young man on the road who had nice eyes, and a nice horse, but who talked too much and was hopeless at changing tires. Anyway, much against the wishes of our families, who all said we were far too young, we got married six months later.

For a short while life seemed so sweet, so perfect. Then came my conscription papers and separation and the long weeks of military training. But I didn't mind that much because it was something we all had to do, and because I knew it would soon be over. I had so much to look forward to, most of all the birth of you. All the talk in the barracks was of war. I think we talked ourselves into this war—perhaps it is always like that.

I came home to see you just once, and now, only a few weeks later, I find myself sitting here in the Malvinas, high in the rocky hills above Stanley Town. Night is coming on and I am waiting for battle.

As I write this, I am so cold I cannot feel my feet. I can hardly hold the pencil I am writing with. The British are coming. They know where we are. They have been bombarding us all day. We cannot see them, but we know they are out there somewhere. We expect them to attack tonight. All of us know in our hearts, though we do not say it, that this will be the last battle. In battle, men die. I do not want to think of that, but it is difficult not to. The officers say we can win, that if we can only hang on, reinforcements will soon be here. But we all know better. They have to say that, don't they?

I can see you now in my head as you were, on the morning I left home. When I looked down upon you that last time, cradled in your mother's arms, I remember I tried to picture you as a

As I write this, I am so cold I cannot feel my feet.

grown boy. I couldn't then, and I still can't. For me you are that sleeping child, yawning toothlessly, fists clenched, frowning through your milk-soaked dreams. But grow up you will, grow up you have, and now that you are old enough, I want to tell you myself how I came to be here, fighting a war in this dreadful place, how I died so far from home. I want to speak to you directly. At least you will know me a little because you can hear my voice in my writing. It is true that I am writing to you also because it helps me—if I think of you I do not think of the battle ahead. I have already written to your mother. She will have read her letter ten years ago now. This is your letter, Carlos, our hello you might call it, and our good-bye.

I had not thought it would end like this. Like all my comrades, I believed what we were told, what we saw on the television, what we read in the papers. The Malvinas belonged to Argentina, and that much is true. They had been stolen from us, they said. We would restore the honor of Argentina and take them back. Our flag would fly again over Stanley. It would be easy, they told us. We would attack in force, overwhelm the British garrison in a few hours. There would be very little shooting. The Malvinas would be ours again, Argentinian, and then we could all go home. I was excited—we all were excited and proud, too, proud that we were the ones chosen to do this for our country. It was all going to be so simple.

And it began well. We came ashore in our landing craft. No one fired a shot at us. As we marched into Stanley, we saw our flag already flying high over the town. The British marines in their green berets sat huddled by the roadside, dejected, defeated. The war was over almost before it had begun. Or so we thought. We had won. The Malvinas were ours again. How the people back home would be cheering, I thought. What heroes we would be when we returned. How we laughed and sang and drank that first night. We did not feel the cold in the wind, not then.

In those early days on the Malvinas, in that first flush of victory, the islands seemed to us like a paradise, a paradise regained. Our paradise. Argentinian.

Yet here I sit only a month or two later and we know that we are about to lose the last battle. The ships did not come. The supplies did not come. Instead the British came, their planes first, then their ships, then their soldiers. We did what we could, Carlos, but we were raw conscripts, poorly fed, poorly equipped, badly led, and we were up against determined fighters. From the moment they sank the great battleship *Belgrano,* the pride of our navy, we knew it could only end one way. I lost my cousin in that ship. I saw men die, good men, my friends, men with wives and mothers and children.

I grew up fast in the terrible weeks that followed. I learned what I should already have understood, that in wars people really do kill one another. I did not hate those I have killed, and those who try to kill me do not hate me either. We are like puppets doing a dance of death, our masters pulling the strings, watched by the world on television. What they don't know is that the puppets are made of flesh, not wood. War, Carlos, has only one result: suffering.

When I heard that the British had landed at San Carlos Bay, I thought of you, and I prayed in the church in Stanley that I would be spared to see you again. They had no candles there. So I went out and bought a box of candles from the store and then I came back and lit them and prayed for me, for you, for your mother. An old lady in a scarf was kneeling at prayer. I saw her watching me as I left. Her eyes met mine and she tried to smile. My English is not that good, but I remember her words. They echo still in my head.

"This is not the way," she said. "It is wrong, wrong."

"Yes," I replied, and left her there.

That was a few days ago now. Since then we have been stuck up here on these freezing hills above Stanley Town, digging in and waiting for the British, who come closer every day. And the bitter wind, from which we cannot hide, chills us to the bone, sapping the last of our strength and most of our courage, too. What courage we have left we shall fight with, but courage will not be enough.

I must finish now. I must fold you away in an envelope and face whatever I must face. As you have grown up, you may not have had a father, but I promise you, you have always had a father's love.

Good-bye, dear Carlos.

And God bless.

Papa ✢

sean rafferty

Sean Rafferty is the least known of the three men who have inspired me to become a writer. Robert Louis Stevenson, of course, I never knew. But he is my friend in a way. Through his books I feel I know him. I long to meet him, to talk to him. Ted Hughes was a friend and my chief mentor. He encouraged me personally, as he did so many young writers, to believe in myself, to go on when the going got tough. Sean was a dear friend, too, and our nearest neighbor for years. He lived simply, selflessly, generously. His death was as remarkable as his life.

It was early one December morning, well before six o'clock. I was still in bed and half asleep when I heard the knock on the door and the sound of a tractor outside. I opened the window. David, our neighboring farmer, was standing there, looking up at me, breathless and pale.

"It's Sean; I think he's dead," he said. "You'd better come, Michael."

I rode with him on the tractor, along the lane and then down the farm track toward the milking parlor, toward Burrow Cottage, where Sean lived, David shouting to me all the time against the noise of the engine about how he'd found Sean in the lane on his way down to milking just minutes before. By now I could see Sean for myself. He was lying there outside the henhouse. I knew he was dead before I even felt how cold he was, before I discovered how stiff he was, how hard to the touch. There was a stillness all around him, no wind in the trees. I remember thinking: Even in death you're in tune with the world, Sean. You died where you belonged. A blackbird piped a requiem from high on the wall of the garden, Sean's garden. I crouched there beside him and wept, my hand on his shoulder. His coat was wet from the rain. He'd fallen like a toy soldier and lay facedown as if at attention, his hat half off, his stick and his right arm trapped underneath him.

I was alone with Sean for a while, waiting for the doctor to come. I talked to him and it didn't seem strange at all. The doctor came mercifully quickly. He spent more time com⁄ forting me than examining the body. "Listen," he said, "here's a man of nearly ninety who's just died the best way you can. I reckon there must be a hundred ways you can go, and believe me, when the time comes, this is the one you would want. Hale and hearty, still living at home, and he just shut down in an instant and keeled over. He'd have known nothing, I prom⁄ ise you. I can tell from the way he fell."

The police came, too—routine they said, because it was a sudden death, and then the ambulance. Sean was taken away. I stood there in the lane watching the ambulance leave, and only then realized I was still holding his hat and his stick. The blackbird was still there, still piping.

Sean Rafferty was in his life a poet, lyricist, playwright, then latterly a publican and a vegetable gardener. He was a man of great wisdom and learning, insightful, sensitive, kind, and above all a gentle spirit. And he was our friend. He had been almost a second father to Clare, my wife, as she grew up. Clare had spent most of her holidays staying with Sean and his wife, Peggy, at the pub they ran together, the Duke of York, in the remote Devon village of Iddesleigh. Here with Christian, Sean's son from his first marriage, Clare first wandered and played in the fields and lanes of Devon, and here she came to love this place and its people. It was her paradise. She would spend her days with Christian, messing about in streams, catching slowworms in the graveyard, talking to foresters and farmers and thatchers, and looking after any animals she could, wild or domestic.

So it was to the same place that she later returned with me and our children to set up Farms for City Children, because she wanted to enable thousands of city children to have the same life-enhancing experience she had had. By now Sean and Peggy were in their seventies and about to retire from the Duke of York. They came to live at Burrow Cottage, nestling in the valley just below Nethercott House, the old Victorian manor house where the children from the cities came to stay for their week down on the farm. But Sean wanted to help. So he worked every day in the walled vegetable garden behind the house, growing vegetables for the children to harvest and eat. And every night he took it upon himself to shut up the hens because he lived nearer to them than us, and besides, he needed the walk up the lane last thing at night—it would be good for him, he said. We knew it wasn't that. It was his way of helping out, that's all.

All this time, Sean was writing, squirreling away his poems in the old oak coffer in his sitting room. Sometimes he would give us one for Christmas, but otherwise he would never talk of his work. He would simply do it quietly. We visited one another often, for Sunday lunch or to share a bottle of wine or two in the evening. And after Peggy died, he came so often he became one of the family. So now he was like a grandfather to us, and the dearest of friends to whom we could confide our hopes and fears, with whom we could talk straight and be ourselves. I have admired no one more, nor has Clare, I think, for Sean was a writer without ego, a generous-hearted man, a great listener with a knowing eye, a flawed and funny man who seemed to have found the inner peace we all yearn for. He lived simply, needing only warmth and whisky and Ryvita and oranges, and Bordeaux wine when we came. He was also the best-read man I have ever met.

He went unrecognized for the most part. He didn't care about that. We did. But he did want his poems collected and published; he wanted them to be there afterward, I think. I remember his joy the day the Carcanet Press contract came, confirming that they would be publishing his collected works. The Bordeaux warmed by his fire down at Burrow tasted so good that evening. He joked often about dying, as we all do, to banish the fear, to postpone the moment. That was the evening he sat back in his chair, glass in hand, and laughed.

"I know how it'll be," he said. "I'll be going up that ruddy lane in the rain one night to see to those ruddy hens, and one of them will still be out as usual, and I'll have to chase it in and shut them up. And then I'll be walking back down the lane and I'll drop dead just there, right outside the henhouse. And the police will come and they'll say: 'Fowl play not suspected.'" And he laughed so much his wine spilled on his trousers.

The collected poems were published, but Sean was dead a year before the book came out.

We had a memorial service up in the church in Iddesleigh. The church was packed. We listened to the music we knew he loved, Mozart especially. Afterward we went back home and drank to him with warm Bordeaux wine from the same glasses in the same room down at Burrow.

He left no instructions as such, but Christian and his family and friends knew he always wanted his ashes to be scattered on the River Milk up in the borders of Scotland, which he loved, where he'd grown up. He'd written of the place, of the event itself even, in one of his poems. Several years before he had written these lines:

Rowan by the red rock, plead,

gean, white gean, in the green holm intercede

for him,

dipper in your flying vestments stay

midstream on the dripping stone to pray

for him

on the first morning of his final day.

And so it happened just as he foretold—he was good at this foretelling. As the ashes blew away and settled softly on the water, as they became a living part of the river, we saw a dipper sitting on a stone in the  middle of the river, and waiting, watching us, waiting for him. ⎯

singing for mrs. pettigrew

I was nearby anyway, so I had every excuse to do it, to ignore the old adage and do something I'd been thinking of doing for many years. "Never go back. Never go back." Those warning words kept repeating themselves in my head as I turned right at the crossroads outside Tillingham and began to walk the few miles along the road back to my childhood home in Bradwell, a place I'd last seen nearly fifty years before. I'd thought of it since, and often. I'd been there in my dreams, seen it so clearly in my mind, but of course I had always remembered it as it had been then. Fifty years would have changed things a great deal, I knew that. But that was part of the reason for my going back that day, to discover how intact the landscape of my memories was.

I wondered if any of the people I had known then might still be there—the three Stebbing sisters perhaps, who lived together in the big house with honeysuckle over the porch—very proper people, so Mother always wanted me to be on my best behavior. It was no more than a stone's throw from the sea and there always seemed to be a gull perched on their chimney pot. I remembered how I'd fallen ignominiously into their goldfish pond and had to be dragged out and dried off by the stove in the kitchen with everyone looking askance at me, and my mother so ashamed. Would I meet Bennie, the village thug who had knocked me off my bike once because I stupidly wouldn't let him have one of my precious lemon drops? Would he still be living there? Would we recognize each other if we met?

The whole silly confrontation came back to me as I walked. If I'd had the wit to surrender just one lemon drop, he probably wouldn't have pushed me, and I wouldn't have fallen into a bramble hedge and had to sit there, humiliated and helpless, as he collected up my entire bagful of scattered lemon drops, shook them triumphantly in my face, and then swaggered off with his cronies, all of them scoffing at me, and scoffing my candy, too. I touched my cheek then as I remembered the huge thorn I had found sticking into it, the point protruding inside my mouth. I could almost feel it again with my tongue, taste the blood. A lot would never have happened if I'd handed over a lemon drop that day.

That was when I thought of Mrs. Pettigrew and her railway car and her dogs and her donkey, and the whole extraordinary story came flooding back crisp and clear, every detail of it, from the moment she found me sitting in the ditch, holding my bleed- ing face and crying my heart out.

She helped me up onto my feet. She would take me to her home. "It isn't far," she said. "I call it Dusit. It is a Thai word which means 'halfway to heaven.'" She had been a nurse in Thailand, she said, a long time ago when she was younger. She'd soon have that nasty thorn out. She'd soon stop it hurting. And she did.

The more I walked, the more vivid it all became: the people, the faces, the whole life of the place where I'd grown up. Everyone in Bradwell seemed to me to have had a very particular character and reputation, unsurprising in a small village, I suppose: Colonel Burton, with his clipped white mustache, who had a wife named Valerie, if I remembered right, with black penciled eyebrows that gave her the look of someone permanently outraged—which she usually was. Neither the colonel nor his wife was to be argued with. They ruled the roost. They would shout at you if you dropped candy wrappers in the village street or rode your bike on the sidewalk.

Mrs. Parsons, whose voice chimed like the bell in her shop when you opened the door, liked to talk a lot. She was a gossip, Mother said, but she was always very kind. She would often slip an extra lemon drop into your paper bag after she had poured your quarter pound from the big glass jar on the counter. I had once thought of stealing that jar, of snatching it and running off out of the shop, making my getaway like a bank robber in the films. But I knew the police would come after me in their shiny black cars with their bells ringing, and then I'd have to go to prison and Mother would be cross. So I never did steal Mrs. Parsons's lemon drop jar.

Then there was Mad Jack, as we called him, who clipped hedges and dug ditches and swept the village street. We'd often see him sitting on the churchyard wall by the mounting block, eating his lunch. He'd be humming and swinging his legs. Mother said he'd been fine before he went off to the war, but he'd come back with some shrapnel from a shell in his head and never been right since, and we shouldn't call him Mad Jack, but we did. I'm ashamed to say we teased him sometimes, too, perching alongside him on the wall, mimicking his humming and swing-ing our legs in time with his.

But Mrs. Pettigrew remained a mystery to everyone. This was partly because she lived some distance from the village and was inclined to keep herself to herself. She came into the village only to go to church on Sundays, and then she'd sit at the back, always on her own. I used to sing in the church choir, mostly because Mother made me, but I did like dressing up in the black cassock and white surplice, and we did have a choir outing once a year to the cinema in Southminster—that's where I first saw *Snow White* and *Bambi* and *Reach for the Sky*. I liked swinging the incense, too, and sometimes I got to carry the cross, which made me feel very holy and very important. I'd caught Mrs. Pettigrew's eye once or twice as we processed by, but I'd always looked away. I'd never spoken to her. She smiled at people, but she rarely spoke to anyone, so no one spoke to her—not that I ever saw, anyway. But there were reasons for this.

Mrs. Pettigrew was different. For a start, she didn't live in a house at all. She lived in a railway car, down by the seawall with the great wide marsh all around her. Everyone called it Mrs. Pettigrew's Marsh. I could see it best when I rode my bicycle along the seawall. The railway car was painted brown and cream and the word PULLMAN was printed in big black letters all along both sides above the windows. There were wooden steps up to the front door at one end, and a chimney at the other. It was surrounded by trees and gardens, so I could only catch occasional glimpses of her

singing for mrs. pettigrew

and her dogs and her donkey, bees, and hens. Tiny under her wide hat, she could often be seen planting out in her vegetable garden, or digging the dyke that ran around the garden like a moat, collecting honey from her beehives, perhaps, or feeding her hens. She was always outside somewhere, always busy. She walked or stood or sat very upright, I noticed, very neatly, and there was a serenity about her that made her unlike anyone else, and ageless, too.

But she was different in another way. Mrs. Pettigrew did not look like the rest of us, because Mrs. Pettigrew was "foreign," from somewhere near China, I had been told. She did not dress like anyone else either. Apart from the wide-brimmed hat, she always wore a long black dress buttoned to the neck. And every-thing about her, her face and her hands, her feet, everything was tidy and tiny and trim, even her voice. She spoke softly to me as she helped me to my feet that day, every word precisely articu-lated. She had no noticeable accent at all, but spoke English far too well, too meticulously, to have come from England.

So we walked side by side, her arm around me, a soothing silence between us, until we turned off the road onto the track that led across the marsh toward the seawall in the distance. I could see smoke rising straight into the sky from the chimney of the railway car.

"There we are: Dusit," she said. "And look who is coming out to greet us."

Three greyhounds were bounding toward us, followed by a donkey trotting purposefully but slowly behind them, wheezing at us rather than braying. Then they were gamboling all about us and nudging us for attention. They were big and bustling, but I wasn't afraid because they had nothing in their eyes but welcome.

"I call the dogs Fast, Faster, and Fastest," she told me. "But the donkey doesn't like names. She thinks names are for silly creatures like people and dogs who can't recognize one another without them. So I call her simply Donkey." Mrs. Pettigrew lowered her voice to a whisper. "She can't bray properly—tries all the time but she can't. She's very sensitive, too—takes offense very easily." Mrs. Pettigrew took me up the steps into her railway car home. "Sit down there by the window, in the light, so I can make your face better."

I was so distracted and absorbed by all I saw about me that I felt no pain as she cleaned my face, not even when she pulled out the thorn. She held it out to show me. It was truly a monster of a thorn. "The biggest and nastiest I have ever seen," she said, smiling at me. Without her hat on she was scarcely taller than I was.

She made me wash out my mouth and bathed the hole in my cheek with antiseptic. Then she gave me some tea that tasted very strange but warmed me to the roots of my hair. "Jasmine tea," she said. "It is very healing, I find, very comforting. My sister sends it to me from Thailand."

The car was as neat and tidy as she was: a simple sitting room at the far end with just a couple of wicker chairs and a small table by the stove. And behind a half-drawn curtain I glimpsed a bed very low on the ground. There was no clutter, no pictures, no hangings, only a shelf of books that ran all the way around the car from end to end. I was sitting at the kitchen table, which looked out over the garden, then through the trees to the open marsh beyond.

"Do you like my house, Michael?" She did not give me time to reply. "I read many books, as you see," she said. I was wondering how it was that she knew my name, when she told me. "I see you in the village sometimes, don't I? You're in the choir, aren't you?" She leaned forward. "And I expect you're wondering why Mrs. Pettigrew lives in a railway car."

"Yes," I said.

The dogs had come in by now and were settling down at our feet, their eyes never leaving her, not for a moment, as if they were waiting for an old story they knew and loved.

"Then I'll tell you, shall I?" she began. "It was because we met on a train, Arthur and I—not this one, you understand, but one very much like it. We were in Thailand. I was returning from my grandmother's house to the city where I lived. Arthur was a botanist. He was traveling through Thailand collecting plants and studying them. He painted them and wrote books about them. He wrote three books; I have them all up there on my shelf. I will show you one day—would you like that? I never knew about plants until I met him, nor insects, nor all the wild creatures and birds around us, nor the stars in the sky. Arthur showed me all these things. He opened my eyes. For me it was all so exciting and new. He had such a knowledge of this wonderful world we live in, such a love for it, too. He gave me that, and he gave me much more: he gave me his love, too.

"Soon after we were married, he brought me here to England on a great ship—this ship had three big funnels and a dance band—and he made me so happy. He said to me one day on board that ship, 'Mrs. Pettigrew'—he always liked to call me this— 'Mrs. Pettigrew, I want to live with you down on the marsh where I grew up as a boy.' The marsh was part of his father's farm, you see. 'It is a wild and wonderful place,' he told me, 'where on calm days you can hear the sea breathing gently beyond the seawall, or on stormy days roaring like a dragon, where larks rise and sing on warm summer afternoons, where stars cascade on August nights.'

"'But where shall we live?' I asked him.

"'I have already thought of that, Mrs. Pettigrew,' he said. 'Because we first met on a train, I shall buy a fine railway car for us to live in, a car fit for a princess. And all around it we shall make a perfect paradise and we shall live as we were meant to live, among our fellow creatures, as close to them as we can be. And we shall be happy there.'

"So we were, Michael. So we were. But only for seventeen short months, until one day there was an accident. We had a generator to make our electricity; Arthur was repairing it when the accident happened. He was very young. That was nearly twenty years ago now. I have been here ever since and I shall always be here. It is just as Arthur told me: a perfect paradise."

Donkey came in just then, clomping up the steps into the railway car, her ears going this way and that. She must have felt she was being ignored or ostracized, probably both. Mrs. Pettigrew shooed her out, but not before there was a terrific kerfuffle of wheezing and growling, of tumbling chairs and crashing crockery.

When I got home, I told Mother everything that had happened. She took me to the doctor at once for a tetanus injection, which hurt much more than the thorn had, then put me to bed and went out—to sort out Bennie, she said. I told her not to, told her it would only make things worse. But she wouldn't listen. When she came back, she brought me a bag of lemon drops. Bennie, she told me, had been marched down to Mrs. Parsons's shop by his father and my mother, and they had made him buy me a bag of lemon drops with his own pocket money to replace the ones he'd stolen from me.

Mother had also cycled out to see Mrs. Pettigrew to thank her for all she had done to help me. From that day on, the two of them became the best of friends, which was wonderful for me because I was allowed to go cycling out to see Mrs. Pettigrew as often as I liked. Sometimes Mother came with me, but mostly I went alone. I preferred it on my own.

I rode Donkey all over the marsh. She needed no halter, no reins. She went where she wanted and I went with her, followed always by Fast, Faster, and Fastest, who would chase rabbits and hares wherever they found them. I was always muddled as to which dog was which, because they all ran unbelievably fast—standing start to full throttle in a few seconds. They rarely caught anything but they loved the chase. With Mrs. Pettigrew I learned how to puff the bees to sleep before taking out the honey-comb. I collected eggs warm from the hens, dug up potatoes, pulled carrots, bottled plums and damsons in Kilner jars. (Ever since, whenever I see the blush on a plum I always think of Mrs. Pettigrew.) And, always, Mrs. Pettigrew would send me home afterward with a present for Mother and me, a pot of honey perhaps or some sweet corn from her garden.

Sometimes Mrs. Pettigrew would take me on a walk along the seawall all the way to Saint Peter's Chapel and back, the oldest chapel in England, she said. Once we stopped to watch a lark rising and rising, singing and singing so high in the blue we could see it no more. But the singing went on, and she said, "I remember a time—we were standing almost on this very same spot—when Arthur and I heard a lark singing just like that. I have never forgotten his words. 'I think it's singing for you,' he said, 'singing for Mrs. Pettigrew.'"

Then there was the night in August when Mother and Mrs. Pettigrew and I lay out on the grass in the garden gazing up at the shooting stars cascading across the sky above us, just as she had with Arthur, she said. How I wondered at the glory of it, and the sheer immensity of the universe. I was so glad then that Bennie had pushed me off my bike that day, so glad I had met Mrs. Pettigrew, so glad I was alive. But soon after came the rumors and the meetings and the anger, and all the gladness was suddenly gone.

I don't remember how I heard about it first. It could have been in the playground at school, or Mother might have told me or even Mrs. Pettigrew. It could have been Mrs. Parsons in the shop. It doesn't matter. One way or another, everyone in the village and for miles around got to hear about it. Soon it was all anyone talked about. I didn't really understand what it meant. It was that first meeting in the village hall that brought it home to me. There were pictures and plans of a giant building pinned up on the wall for everyone to see. There was a model of it, too, with the marsh all around and the seawall running along behind it, and the blue sea beyond with models of fishing boats and yachts sailing by. That, I think, was when I truly began to comprehend the implication of what was going on, of what was actually being proposed. The men in suits sitting behind the table on the platform that evening made it quite clear.

They wanted to build a power station, but not just an ordinary power station, a huge newfangled atomic power station, the most modern design in the whole world, they said. They had decided to build it out on the marsh—and everyone knew by now they meant Mrs. Pettigrew's Marsh. It was the best place, they said. It was the safest place, they said, far enough outside the village and far enough away from London. I didn't understand then who the men in suits were, of course, but I did understand what they were telling us: that this atomic power station was necessary because it would provide cheaper electricity for all of us; that London, which was only fifty or so miles away, was growing fast and needed more electricity. Bradwell had been chosen because it was the perfect site, near the sea so the water could be used for cooling, and near to London, but not too near.

"If it's for Londoners, and if it's so safe, what's wrong with it being right in London then?" the colonel asked.

"They've got water there, too, haven't they?" said Miss Blackwell, my teacher.

Mrs. Parsons stood up then, beside herself with fury. "Well, I think they want to build it out here miles away from London because it might blow up like that bomb in Hiroshima. That's what I think. I think it's wicked, wicked. And anyway, what about Mrs. Pettigrew? She lives out there on the marsh. Where's she going to live?"

Beside me Mother was holding Mrs. Pettigrew's hand and patting it as the argument raged on. There'd be any number of new jobs, said one side. There are plenty of jobs, anyway, said the other side. It would be a great concrete monstrosity; it would blight the whole landscape. It would be well screened by trees, well landscaped; you'd hardly notice it; and, anyway, you'd get used to it soon enough once it was there. It would be clean, too, no chimneys, no smoke. But what if there was an accident, if the radiation leaked out? What then?

Suddenly Mrs. Pettigrew was on her feet. Maybe it was because she didn't speak for a while that everyone fell silent around her. When she did speak at last, her voice trembled. It trembled because she was trembling, her knuckles bone-white as she clutched Mother's hand. I can still remember what she said, almost word for word.

"Since I first heard about this, I have read many books. From these books I have learned many important things. At the heart of an atomic power station there is a radioactive core. The energy this core makes produces electricity. But this energy has to be used and controlled with very great care. Any mistake or any accident could cause this radioactive core to become unstable. This could lead to an explosion, which would be catastrophic, or there could be a leak of radiation into the atmosphere. Either of these would cause the greatest destruction to all forms of life: human beings, animals, birds, sea life, and plants, for miles and miles around. But I am sure those who wish to build this power station have thought of all this and will make it as safe as possible. I am sure those who will operate it will be careful. But Arthur, my late husband, was careful, too. He installed a simple generator for our home. He thought it was safe, but it killed him.

"So I ask you, gentlemen, to think again. Machines are not perfect. Science is not perfect. Mistakes can easily be made. Accidents can happen. I am sure you understand this. And there is something else I would like you to understand. For me the place where you would build your atomic power station is home. You may have decided it is an uninteresting place and unimportant, just home to one strange lady who lives there on the marsh with her donkey and her dogs and her hens. But it is not uninteresting and it is not unimportant. It is not just my home, either, but home also for curlews and gulls and wild geese and teal and redshanks and barn owls and kestrels. There are herons and larks. The otter lives here and the fox comes to visit, the badger, too, even sometimes the deer. And among the marsh grass and reeds and the bulrushes live a thousand different insects, and a thousand different plants. My home is their home, too, and you have no right to destroy it. Arthur called the marsh a perfect paradise. But if you build your atomic power station there, then this paradise will be destroyed forever. You will make a hell of paradise."

Her voice gained ever greater strength as she spoke. Never before or since have I heard anyone speak with greater conviction.

"And I do mean forever," she went on. "Do not imagine that in fifty years, or a hundred maybe, when this power station will have served its purpose, when they find a new and better way to make electricity—which I am quite sure they will—do not imagine that they will be able to knock it down and clear it away and the marsh will be once again as it is now. From my books I know that no building as poisonous with radiation as this will ever be knocked down. To stop the poison leaking, it will, I promise you, have to be enclosed in a tomb of concrete for hundreds of years to come. This they do not want to tell you, but it is true, believe me. Do not, I beg you, let them build this power station. Let us keep this marsh as it is. Let us keep our perfect paradise."

As she sat down, there was a ripple of applause, which swiftly became tumultuous. And as the hall rang loud with cheering and whistling and stamping, I joined in more enthusiastically than any. At that moment I felt the entire village was united in defiance behind her. But the applause ended, as—all too soon—did both the defiance and the unity.

The decision to build or not to build seemed to take forever—more public meetings, endless campaigning for and against—but right from the start, it was clear to me that those for it were always in the ascendant. Mother stood firm alongside Mrs. Pettigrew; so did the colonel and Mrs. Parsons, but Miss Blackwell soon changed sides, as did lots of others. The arguments became ever more bitter. People who had been perfectly friendly until now would not even speak to one another. At school Bennie led an ever-growing gang who would storm about at playtime, punching their fists in the air and chanting slogans. "Down with the Pettigrew weeds!" they cried. "Down with the Pettigrew weeds!" To my shame I slunk away and avoided them all I could.

But in the face of this angry opposition, Mother did not flinch and neither did Mrs. Pettigrew. They sat side by side at every meeting, stood outside the village hall in the rain with their ever dwindling band of supporters, holding up their placard. SAY NO TO THE POWER STATION it read. Sometimes after school I stood there with them, but when people began to swear at us out of their car windows as they passed by, Mother said I had to stay away. I wasn't sorry. It was boring to stand there, and cold, too, in spite of the warmth of the brazier. And I was always terrified whenever Bennie saw me there, because I knew I'd be his special target in the playground the next day.

Eventually there were just the two of them left, Mother and

Mrs. Pettigrew. Mad Jack would join them sometimes, because he liked the company and he liked warming his hands over the brazier, too. Things became even nastier toward the end. I came out of the house one morning to find red paint daubed on our front door and our Bramley apple tree, the one I used to climb, and someone—I always thought it must have been Bennie—threw a stone through one of Mrs. Pettigrew's windows in the middle of the night. Mother and Mrs. Pettigrew did what they could to keep each other's spirits up, but they could see the way it was going, so it must have been hard.

Then one day it was in the newspapers. The plans for the atomic power station had been approved. Building would begin in a few months. Mother cried a lot about it at home and I expect Mrs. Pettigrew did, too, but whenever I saw them together, they always tried to be cheerful. Even after Mrs. Pettigrew received the order that her beloved marsh was being compulsorily purchased and that she would have to move out, she refused to be down-hearted. We'd go over there even more often toward the end to be with her, to help her in her garden with her bees and her hens and her vegetables. She was going to keep the place just as Arthur had liked it, she said, for as long as she possibly could.

Then Donkey died. We arrived one day to find Mrs. Pettigrew

singing for mrs. pettigrew

sitting on the steps of her railway car, Donkey lying nearby. We helped her dig the grave. It took hours. When Donkey had been buried, we all sat on the steps in the half-dark, the dogs lying by Donkey's grave. The sea sighed behind the seawall, perfectly reflecting our spirits. I was lost in sadness.

"There's a time to die," said Mrs. Pettigrew. "Perhaps she knew it was her time." I never saw Mrs. Pettigrew smile again.

I was there, too, on the day of the auction. Mrs. Pettigrew didn't have much to sell, but a lot of people came along all the same, out of curiosity or even a sense of malicious triumph, per-haps. The car had been emptied of everything—I'd carried some of it out myself—so that the whole garden was strewn with all her bits and pieces. It took just a couple of hours for the auction-eer to dispose of everything. all the garden tools, all the furniture, all the crockery, the generator, the stove, the pots and pans, the hens and the henhouse and the beehives. She kept only her books and her dogs, and the railway car, too. Several buyers wanted to make a bid for it, but she refused. She stood stony-faced through-out, Mother at her side, while I sat watching everything from the steps of the car, the dogs at my feet.

Neither Mother nor I had any idea what she was about to do. Evening was darkening around us, I remember. Just the three of us were left there. Everyone else had gone. Mother was leading Mrs. Pettigrew away, a comforting arm around her, telling her again that she could stay with us in the village as long as she liked, as long as it took to find somewhere else to live. But Mrs. Pettigrew didn't appear to be listening at all. Suddenly she stopped, turned, and walked away from us back toward the car.

"I won't be long," she said. And when the dogs tried to fol-low her, she told them to sit where they were and stay.

She disappeared inside and I thought she was just saying good-bye to her home, but she wasn't. She came out a few moments later, shutting the door behind her and locking it.

I imagined at first it was the reflection of the last of the setting sun glowing in the windows. Then I saw the flicker of flames and realized what she had done. We stood there together and watched as the car caught fire, as it blazed and roared and crack-led, the flames running along under the roof, leaping out of the windows, as the sparks flurried and flew. The fire engines came, but too late. The villagers came, but too late. How long we stood there I do not know, but I know that I ached with crying.

Mrs. Pettigrew came and lived with us at home for a few months. She hardly spoke in all that time. In the end she left us her dogs and her books to look after and went back to Thailand to live with her sister. We had a few letters from her after that, then a long silence, then the worst possible news from her sister.

Mrs. Pettigrew had died, of sadness, of a broken heart, she said.

Mother and I moved out of the village a year or so later, as the power station was being built. I remember the trucks rumbling through, and the Irish laborers who had come to build it sitting on the church wall with Mad Jack and teaching him their songs.

Mother didn't feel it was the same place anymore, she told me. She didn't feel it was safe. But I knew she was escaping from sadness. We both were. I didn't mind moving, not one bit.

As I walked into the village, I could see now the great gray hulk of the power station across the fields. The village was much as I remembered it, only smarter, more manicured. I made straight for my childhood home. The house looked smaller, prettier, and tidier, too, the garden hedge neatly clipped; the garden itself, from what I could see from the road, looked too well groomed, not a nettle in sight. But the Bramley apple tree was still there, still leaning sideways as if it were about to fall over. I thought of knocking on the door, of asking if I might have a look inside at my old bedroom where I'd slept as a child. But a certain timidity and a growing uneasiness that coming back had not been such a

We stood there together and watched as the car caught fire.

good idea prevented me from doing it. I was beginning to feel that by being there I was tampering with memories, yet now that I was there, I could not bring myself to leave.

I spoke to a postman emptying the postbox and inquired about some of the people I'd known. He was a good age, in his fifties, I thought, but he knew no one I asked him about. Mad Jack wasn't on his wall. Mrs. Parsons's shop was still there but now sold antiques and bric-a-brac. I went to the churchyard and found the graves of the colonel and his wife with the black penciled eyebrows, but I'd remembered her name wrong. She was Veronica, not Valerie. They had died within six months of each other. I got to chatting with the man who had just finished mowing the grass in the graveyard and asked him about the atomic power station and whether people minded living alongside it.

"Course I mind," he replied. He took off his flat cap and wiped his brow with his forearm. "Whoever put that ruddy thing up should be ashamed of themselves. Never worked properly all the time it was going, anyway."

"It's not going anymore then?" I asked.

"Been shut down, I don't know, maybe eight or nine years," he said, waxing even more vehement. "Out of date. Clapped out. Useless. And do you know what they had to do? They had to wrap the whole place under a blanket of concrete, and it's got to stay there like that for a couple of hundred years at least so's it doesn't leak out and kill the lot of us. Madness, that's what it was, if you ask me. And when you think what it must have been like before they put it up. Miles and miles of wild marshland as far as the eye could see. All gone. Must've been wonderful. Some funny old lady lived out there in a railway car. Chinese lady, they say. And she had a donkey. True. I've seen photos of her and some kid sitting on a donkey outside her railway car. Last person to live out there, she was. Then they went and kicked her out and built that ugly great wart of a place. And for what? For a few years of electricity that's all been used up and gone. Price of progress, I suppose they'd call it. I call it a crying shame."

I bought a card in the post office and wrote a letter to Mother. I knew she'd love to hear I'd been back to Bradwell. Then I made my way past the Cricketers' Inn and the school, where I stopped to watch the children playing where I'd played, then on toward Saint Peter's, the old chapel by the seawall, the favorite haunt of my youth, where Mrs. Pettigrew had taken me all those years before, remote and bleak from the outside, and inside filled with quiet and peace. Some new houses had been built along the road since my time. I hurried past, trying not to notice them, longing now to leave the village behind me. I felt that my memories had been trampled enough.

One house name on a white-painted gate to a new bungalow caught my eye: New Clear View. I saw the joke, but didn't feel like smiling. And beyond the bungalow, there it was again, the power station, massive now because I was closer, a monstrous complex of buildings rising from the marsh, malign and immovable. It offended my eye. It hurt my heart. I looked away and walked on.

When I reached the chapel, no one was there. I had the place to myself, which was how I had always liked it. After I had been inside, I came out and sat down with my back against the sun-warmed brick and rested. The sea murmured. I remembered again my childhood thoughts, how the Romans had been here, the Saxons, the Normans, and now me. A lark rose then from the grass below the seawall, rising, rising, singing, singing. I watched it disappear into the blue, still singing, singing for Mrs. Pettigrew. ✣

key dates for michael

1943   Born in St. Albans, England

1944   Evacuated to Cumberland

1947   Lived in Philbeach Gardens, London

1948   Attended St. Matthias CE Primary School, Warwick
Road

1951   Attended Abbey Preparatory School, Forest Row

1952   Moved to Bradwell-on-Sea (Bradwell-Juxta-Mare), Essex

1957   Attended King's School, Canterbury

1962   Spent year at Royal Military Academy, Sandhurst

1963   Married Clare Lane (daughter of Allen Lane, founder of
Penguin Books)
Living in Rogate, West Sussex
Started teaching in preparatory school
Met Sean Rafferty
Began travels to France

1964   First son, Sebastian, born
Began writing short stories

1965   Moved to London
Studied at King's College London

1967	Moved to Buriton then Froxfield, Hampshire
	Second son, Horatio, born
1968	Moved to Cambridge
	Daughter, Rosalind, born
1970	Allen Lane, father-in-law, died
	Moved to Kent
	Taught in junior and primary schools
1971	*Children's Words* published by the National Book League
1974	Published collection of short stories
1975	Bought farm and moved to Devon
1976	Started Farms for City Children
	First children visited Nethercott
	Met Ted and Carol Hughes
1977	*Friend or Foe* published
1978–84	Vacationed in Zennor, Cornwall
1982	*War Horse* published (1983 in U.S.)
1984	Began visiting Bryher, Isles of Scilly
1985	*Why the Whales Came* published (U.K. and U.S.)
1986	First grandchild, Léa, born. Followed since then by Eloise, Alice, Lucie, Alan, Laurence, and Hazel
1987	Visited Oradour-sur-Glane
1988	Filming of *Why the Whales Came*

1990–2000	*The Butterfly Lion, King of the Cloud Forests, The Wreck of the Zanzibar, Waiting for Anya, The Dancing Bear,* and other titles published
1992–95	Bosnian War
1993	Mother died Sean Rafferty died
1998	Created Children's Laureate with Ted Hughes
1999	*Kensuke's Kingdom* and "My Father Is a Polar Bear" published (2003 in U.S.)
2001	Foot and mouth disease outbreak; all farms closed for eight months *Out of the Ashes* published
2003	*Private Peaceful* published (2004 in U.S.) Appointed as third Children's Laureate
2004–05	Traveled extensively in Russia, South Africa, Europe, and all over British Isles *The Best Christmas Present in the World* published
2005	Spent two weeks in Venice *I Believe in Unicorns* and *The Amazing Story of Adolphus Tips* published (both 2006 in U.S.)
2006	*Singing for Mrs. Pettigrew* published (2009 in U.S.)
2007	*The Mozart Question* published (2008 in U.S.)